Budapest

- A ☞ in the text denotes a highly recommended sight
- A complete A–Z of practical information starts on p.104
- Extensive mapping on cover flaps

Berlitz Publishing Company, Inc.

Princeton   Mexico City   Dublin   Eschborn   Singapore

Original Text:	Paul Murphy
Photography:	Byron Russell, Berlitz Publishing
Editors:	Media Content Marketing, Inc.
Layout:	Media Content Marketing, Inc.
Cartography:	GeoSystems Global Corporation

Although we make every effort to ensure the accuracy of all information in this book, changes do occur. If you find an error in this guide, please let our editors know by writing to us at Berlitz Publishing Company, 400 Alexander Park, Princeton, NJ 08540-6306. A postcard will do.

ISBN 2-8315-6955-9
Revised 1998 – First Printing November 1998

Printed in Italy
019/811 REV

CONTENTS

Budapest

BUDAPEST AND THE HUNGARIANS

The story of Budapest is a tale of two, or even three, cities. Until 1873 Budapest as such did not exist—there were just the separate entities of Buda, Pest, and Obuda (Old Buda)—that it might be said Budapest is one of the youngest capitals in Europe. However, the city's history goes back thousands of years, to even before the Romans arrived and set up an outpost to defend their empire against the barbarians from the east. Althought the Roman empire crumbled, as successive waves of people invaded and settled the land, the city of Buda did not.

It was not until the ninth century that a nation rose out of the chaos, and by the 15th century Buda was a rich centre of learning and culture, crowned by a spectacular royal palace. But the country's problems were only just beginning. Invasion, occupation, revolution, and war characterize Hungarian history, and the people of Budapest have seen their city emerge from this disarray and then fall time and time again.

The 20th century has been no different—twice Hungary entered world wars and twice it ended on the losing side. In 1948 Soviet rule was imposed on a broken land, and a popular uprising in 1956 was ferociously crushed. Looking up in many parts of the city, one sees how the pock-marked buildings still bear the scars of many of these conflicts. Today, however, as Hungary is poised to enter NATO, the future looks decidedly brighter..

"I like that Coca Cola sign," the tour guide said to us, pointing above as the coach rumbled through Obuda. "I don't drink Coca Cola—I don't like what Coca Cola stands for—but I like the sign." We looked at her blankly. "You see," she explained, "in the past there used to be a hammer and sickle there." Today there's little such Soviet paraphernalia left in the streets of Budapest. Avenues and squares have been, or are being, renamed, and the effigies of Lenin, Marx, and Engels have been hidden away in a new statue park (see box opposite).

It was, in fact, Hungary that first tore back the Iron Curtain in 1989 beginning the momentous chain of events that ended Communitst dominance in Central and Eastern Europe. Communism's demise has allowed present-day Hungarians to look toward a different future, one that holds much promise.

The transition to full capitalism in Hungary has been a little more gradual, and therefore easier, than that in other former Eastern bloc states, as the country has always enjoyed a limited form of it. The most visible signs of increasingwealth are the Mercedes and BMWs replacing Trabants and Skodas on the street. The proliferation of American fast-food outlets also signals the embrace of a certain part of Western culture.

The city has learned Western pricing too, and visitors

will receive an unpleasant surprise if they presume that all accommodation in Central Europe must be relatively cheap. Budapest's four- and five-star hotels are now almost as costly as

Embroidered and hand-spun blouses such as this one are part of the folk-art tradition in Budapest.

those in the West. The good news for the visitor, however, is that many daily necessities are still priced for the benefit of the Hungarians: the highly commendable public transport system; hearty food and drink served in the *borozó* (wine bar) or *söröző* (beer hall); coffee and cakes in elegant Victorian coffee-houses; and museums.

With a population reaching two and a half million, which is ten times the size of the country's next biggest town, it would be incorrect to underestimate the importance of Budapest to the country. It is the political, industrial, economic and cultural centre, and is home to 20 percent of the Hungarian people.

Szobor (Statue) Park

Possibly Budapest's most curious attraction, Szobor Park was opened in September 1993. Statues relating to people and events no longer "politically correct" have been removed from their sites in Budapest, and some other cities as well, to what has been termed a "communist theme park" deep in the Buda suburbs.

Here stand the kind of heroic Eastern bloc agitprop statues Westerners may recognize from old posters or postage stamps. Lenin, Marx, and Engels are all here, but are by no means the stars of this collection of more than 40 monuments dating from 1948 to as recently as 1986. It's a fascinating example of the rewriting of modern history.

Szobor Park is in the XXIII district on the corner of *Balatoni út* and *Szabadkai út*, about 45 minutes by bus from the city centre. You won't find the location on any map of central Budapest, however, so ask Tourinform for directions. It is open between April and October from 10:00 A.M. to 6:00 P.M. Monday–Friday, 8:00 A.M. to dusk on weekends; between November and March it is open just Saturday and Sunday from 8:00 A.M. to dusk.

It also has by far the most attractions for visitors. Chief among these is Buda's Castle Hill, an area which has suffered 31 sieges and has been reduced to rubble on several occasions. Yet enough of it remains, or has been rebuilt, to constitute one of Europe's most charming medieval enclaves. Pest, on the other hand, is a remarkably complete example of late 19th-century town planning, with sweeping monumental avenues and bold Art Nouveau and Neo-Baroque buildings. Many streets and squares retain a grand *fin-de-siècle* Middle European atmosphere and it is easy to see why Budapest has often been called "the Paris of the East."

The similarity with Paris doesn't stop at the architecture. Budapest is a hedonistic city. There is no shortage of bars and *bierstubes*, each luxury hotel has its own nightclub, and casinos are flourishing. But the city's most acclaimed offerings are in opera and classical music performances. There is no class division among audiences at these events in Budapest, and tickets are priced to accommodate the locals as well as the comparatively rich tourists. The beautiful Opera House is rated among the finest in Europe, while the tradition of Liszt lives on in the concert halls.

However, the city has some unique pleasure domes that have been here far longer. Budapest's steam baths (*fürdő*) are world-renowned, and people bathe in the hot mineral water for pleasure as well as for medicinal purposes. While wealthy westerners take to the thermal baths in the luxury hotels on and around Margaret Island, the locals are soaking and socializing for just a few forints beneath ancient stone domes left by the Turks. There really is no better way to relax from city life than in a *fürdő*. If you want to swim off those extra calories, there are some fine swimming pools here as well.

Eating out in Budapest has come a long way in the past decade. During the 1980s the government gave up its monopoly on eating places and the uninspired cooking of the communist canteen was banished forever. Nowadays several of the city's restaurants are famous across Central Europe and some are even among the best in Europe. Inevitably prices have risen with the increase in quality, but the inexpensive, authentic Hungarian eating-houses still exist.

Just out of town, a trip to the Buda Hills is a must for the exhilarating views and fresh air, while farther afield the old towns of the Danube Bend are so pretty and easily accessible from the capital that you might suspect the tourist board had planned it that way. Szentendre is a picturesque artists' colony in an 18th-century time warp, while Esztergom and Visegrád hold more of the ancient and weighty treats: remains of formidable medieval castles and palaces, and the

The Chain Bridge, opened in 1849, was the first span to unite Buda and Pest.

Essential goulash ingredients: garlic and paprika for sale at the old covered market.

country's largest church and finest religious art collection. And when you see the views of the river from Visegrád, you'll surely understand why Strauss devoted a waltz to the Danube, even if he did take a bit of artistic licence in describing its colour.

If you want to turn your Budapest trip into a seaside holiday, then head for Lake Balaton, Central Europe's biggest lake and the next best thing to the sea. The south shore caters to family holiday-makers and the north has plenty to offer outdoor and culture enthusiasts.

You needn't worry about the language problem, and there's certainly no attitude problem. The friendly Hungarians are now diligently learning English and German, and are even more diligently forgetting what little Russian they may have known. English is widely understood in the Castle Hill area and inner city Pest, and you can get along quite well elsewhere if you speak a little German. Although the Hungarians don't expect you to speak their language, it doesn't hurt for visitors to try out a few phrases in Hungarian. Besides, the Budapestis are renowned for their hospitality and generally welcome tourists for more than just their hard currency.

A new era is dawning in Budapest as the city emerges from the Soviet shadow and takes greater control of its destiny. Yet, although the city has reawakened in modern Europe, a proud sense of the past pervades its older parts, which bear witness to the stubborn progress of the nation towards its new-found freedom.

A BRIEF HISTORY

By European standards, the Hungarians are relative new-comers. They have lived in the Carpathian Basin for a mere 1,100 years—but during that time they've had more than their share of suffering.

Early Settlers

The settlement of present-day Hungary goes far back in time. Less than 64 km (40 miles) to the west of Budapest, human traces thought to be half a million years old have been excavated and are now on display at the Hungarian National Museum. The first tribes that came to this area brought skills and tools which improved the lot of the hunter, made farming feasible, and, in time, gave rise to primitive industries.

Around the third century B.C., Hungary was occupied by a Celtic-Illyrian tribe known as Eraviscans, refugees from wars in Greece. They established a tribal centre on top of Gellért Hill and continued the early settlers' artistic and industrial innovations.

The Roman Empire

Hungary remained beyond the reach of western Europe until the first century A.D., when the Roman empire's legions advanced and pushed its northeast frontier to the Danube. By the second century, about 20,000 Roman troops were deployed along the river between Vienna and Budapest.

To command and coordinate this long, exposed line, the Romans built a military camp called Aquincum, which became the home of some 6,000 soldiers, and in time spawned civilian suburbs that housed up to ten times that number. In A.D. 106 Aquincum was made the capital of the Roman empire's province of Lower Pannonia, and its amphitheatres, bathing complexes, aqueducts, and the sheer size and quality of the remains unearthed in present-day Obuda testify to its former importance.

As the Roman empire began to crumble, however, Huns and Vandals swarmed over the river, and during the early fifth century Aquincum fell to the tribes of Attila. It is believed that the town on the west side of the river was named after Attila's brother (or possibly his brother-in-law), Buda, who was banished there. When Attila died in 453 the Huns were overthrown and the Avars became the dominant power, occupying the region from the middle of the sixth century to the early ninth century.

The First Hungarians

The tribes that were ultimately to settle in the land arrived in 896. They had wandered a long way from their home east of the Ural Mountains, and fell upon the land with such ferocity that the local people thought they too were Huns (one might be tempted to think this is the origin of the English *Hungary*).

But they were actually Magyars (the Hungarian word for Hungarians); their language was strange to outsiders. The tribe's name for itself became the name of the country and its language, as well. Related tribes, who had earlier travelled northwest while the Magyars migrated west, ended up in Finland. Their mutually incomprehensible tongues are classified together in the linguistic field as Finno-Ugric.

The first leader of the Magyars, Prince Arpád, founded a dynasty that lasted more than three centuries and introduced statehood to the new land. Prince Géza, his great-grandson, embraced Christianity, and on the legendary date of Christmas Day A.D. 1000, Géza's son, Steven (István), later St. Stephen (Szent István), was crowned the first king of Hungary in the city of Esztergom, situated on the Danube Bend.

Figures from Hungary's past form an imposing backdrop for Heroes' Square.

The first record of Pest, meaning "lime furnace" or "ovens" in Slavic, comes from 1061. A landmark of the nation's civilization in these early days, the Golden Bull of 1222 was a sort of "Magyar Carta" spelling out the rights of nobles and commoners alike. But the rights of man were the last thing on the minds of the Mongols, who overran the country in 1241 and again in 1242. Whole towns and villages, including Buda and Pest, were subjected to an orgy of killing and destruction. The Mongols did not stay, however, nor did they return. King Béla IV then set about reviving the wrecked nation, and founded the town of Buda, wisely building it within fortified walls.

The Angevin Dynasty

The Arpád dynasty ended in 1301; the French House of Angevin (Anjou), in the shape of Károly (Charles) Róbert, claimed the crown. He moved the court to Visegrád before it came permanently to Buda's Castle Hill.

Two more foreign kings ruled after Róbert, but it was a Hungarian noble, János Hunyadi, who was to become the

A fixture in Heroes' Square: the statue of the enlightened King Matthias.

national saviour in the mid-15th century. The Turks had been threatening the country for some time but Hunyadi led the Hungarian army to victory against them at Nándorfehérvár (now Belgrade) in 1456.

The son of János Hunyadi, Korvin Mátyás (Matthias Corvinus), ascended the throne in 1458 and for the next 32 years the country enjoyed a golden age of intellectual and civic development. Under this enlightened king's rule, the city of Buda became an advanced centre of Renaissance culture and Pest flourished in trade and industry. King Mátyás' Royal Palace was the talk of Europe.

Hungarians say that when Mátyás died so did justice, resulting in internal strife. Despotic noblemen repressed the peasants so harshly that an army led by György Dózsa rose in rebellion in 1514, but the insurrection failed; Dózsa was roasted alive and the serfs' condition continued to decline.

Meanwhile the Turks were again massing for war. This time there was no Hunyadi to lead the weakened nation, and the king, Lajos (Louis) II, and much of his army were killed at the battle of Mohács (in southern Hungary) in 1526.

The neighbouring Austrian Habsburg rulers, fearful that Vienna would be the Ottoman empire's next conquest, proclaimed themselves rulers of Hungary, thus creating a buffer zone between themselves and the Turks. Hungary was effectively dismembered: the north and west fell to the Habsburgs; Transylvania became a so-called independent principality under Turkish auspices; and central Hungary came under direct Turkish rule. The Turks finally occupied Buda in 1541 and stayed there for almost a century and a half, achieving and bequeathing little of note except, of course, their baths.

By the late 17th century the Christian armies of the West were fully mobilized against the Ottoman infidels. Long, devastating sieges were laid to both Buda and Pest and, when finally liberated in 1686, the cities once again lay in ruins.

Under the Habsburgs

The Hungarian people then found themselves under the rule of the Habsburgs, which was not much better than life under the pashas, and in 1703 Prince Ferenc Rákóczi led an eight-year struggle for independence. Outnumbered and deserted by their French allies, the Hungarians finally lost the war in 1711.

Peace lasted for the rest of the century and the country made great economic strides as a province of the Habsburg

---

The Turul Bird

On top of Castle Hill, by the funicular railway, a great bronze condor-like bird looks out over the city from its perch on the ornamental railings of the Royal Palace. This is the mythical turul bird which, according to legend, was the father of Almos, whose son Arpád led the Magyar tribes into Hungary.

Some stories also tell of how turul birds guided the tribes on their long voyage from north Europe to their new homeland.

Budapest has few reminders of this colourful legend; the only other place you will see turul birds is on top of the pillars of the Szabadság híd (Liberty Bridge).

---

empire. Factories, theatres, and newspapers were opened and Pest expanded its role in international trade while Buda regained its status as Hungary's administrative centre.

But prosperity was not for the majority. The rich were getting richer while the serfs were getting poorer, and the Magyar identity was being repressed by the influence of

An artist's conception of a Magyar saga on display in the Hungarian National Gallery.

the Germanic Habsburgs. In the mid-19th century, the Hungarians once again went to war for their independence.

The rebellion of 1848 was led by a group of young intellectuals, including the 25-year-old radical poet, Sándor Petőfi. A provisional government was formed, headed by Lajos Kossuth, but it was short-lived. The Emperor Franz Joseph I summoned help from the Czar of Russia and the revolt was crushed in 1849.

All was not totally lost, however. In 1867, under a compromise designed to curtail home-rule agitation, the Austro-Hungarian empire was established and Hungary was finally granted its own government, though key ministries were shared with the Austrians. This "Dual Monarchy" saw out the 19th century on a bright note, with splendid boulevards and proud buildings erected to create the Pest we recognize today. The Chain Bridge became the first permanent link across the river, the Pest metro and the Pest-Vienna railway opened, and, in 1873, the towns of Pest, Buda, and Obuda merged to become Budapest.

Wars and Revolutions

In 1914, as part of the Austro-Hungarian empire, Hungary was called upon to enter World War I. Their involvement in the war cost many thousands of Hungarian lives, and the country's hardships multiplied.

In October 1918, Hungary's last king, Károly IV, was toppled by what is now called the Bourgeois Democratic Revolution. The revolutionaries joined with the newly-born Hungarian communist movement, but took their reform demands too far and too fast, and only succeeded in provoking a right-wing backlash led by Admiral Miklós Horthy.

Meanwhile, the aftermath of war, as dictated by the 1920 Treaty of Trianon, was to cost Hungary very dearly. About two-thirds of the country, including the traditional homeland of Transylvania, was handed over to the new "Successor States"—Romania, Yugoslavia, and Czechoslovakia. Horthy maintained his role as regent in the grim twenties and thirties while the country, demoralized and impoverished, seethed over the treaty.

Hitler's Germany, meanwhile, provided investment in Hungarian industry and a market for Hungarian farm produce, and earned a grudging admiration from the Hungarians for its defiance of the World War I allies. In 1940 Hungary allowed the German army to cross its territory and, as a reward, they temporarily recovered parts of its former lands from Romania and Yugoslavia. It was a false dawn before the country's blackest hours. Thousands of Hungarians died supporting the Germans on the Russian Front, and just as Horthy thought he could squirm out of Hitler's grasp by declaring neutrality in 1944, the country was occupied by the Germans.

The Pengö in Your Pocket

Although many people have heard of the incredible hyperinflation suffered by Germany in the days after World War I, it is not as well known that Hungary holds the dubious record for the world's worst inflation. For every one pengő (the unit of currency which preceded the forint) owned before the war it was necessary to own 1.4 billion after the war, just to keep pace. In 1946 there were Hungarian bank notes in circulation worth a mind-boggling 100 million million million pengős.

As a corollary to this, the most worthless stamp ever issued by a country was the Hungarian 3,000 pengő stamp of 1946. At the time one British penny would have purchased 50,000 million of these.

As the Soviet army moved closer to Budapest in late 1944 and the bombing of the city became more intense, Horthy played his last card by declaring an armistice. The Germans responded by installing in power a Hungarian fascist group called the Arrow Cross. This brutal, fanatical regime murdered hundreds of Budapestis and ensured further destruction of the city by fighting the Red Army to the death. By the time the Russians finally took Budapest, three-quarters of its buildings were demolished and the Hungarian death toll in the war came to about half a million.

Booksellers and other vendors display their goods on the street in Old Town.

In and Out of the Red

Post-war Hungary was transformed from a republic (1946) into a People's Republic (1949). Life under the Soviets was not much brighter than existence under the Nazis. After a hopeful democratic beginning with free elections, fear and turbulence ensued. Stalin's man, Mátyás Rákosi, established his sinister AVO secret police to ensure compliance with party doctrine.

After eight years of often brutal repression the people had had enough and, on 23 October 1956, marched on Parliament to air their grievances. The students and workers were met with police bullets. The protest snowballed into a popular uprising and within days a provisional Hungarian government, led by Imre Nagy, had withdrawn from the Warsaw Pact. Soviet retribution took just 12 days. On 4 November, Red Army tanks entered Budapest and quickly crushed the armed resistance. The West watched in horror as Nagy and thousands more were executed. Some 200,000 Hungarians fled the country.

The Soviets installed János Kádár as the new party boss. Although rule began in repressive fashion, gradually, by the mid-1960s, severe ideological doctrines were being relaxed. Hungarians embraced a form of consumerism; they were allowed to take holidays in the West (though limited to once every three or four years, and not to every Western country), and the "goulash economy," even though it failed to meet its potential, was held up as a model in the Eastern bloc.

As the winds of perestroika blew in from Moscow, Kádár was removed from power in 1988, and, in 1989, the formation of opposition parties was legalized. Hungary was the first country to draw back its Iron Curtain, dismantling the barbed wire along its Austrian border and allowing East Germans to escape to the West. In 1990 the country held its first free elections in 43 years and was called a republic again; in 1991 it became an associate member of the European Community. In 1997 Hungary was offered membership in the NATO.

The transition from communism to capitalism has not been easy, as all the former Eastern bloc states have found, but Hungary, at least, has a significant share of Western investments to help support its rather fragile economy. As a bridge between East and West Europe it is well positioned for any improvement in trade between the two geo-political blocks. Its hopes for the future are full membership of the European Union and two things rare in the history of Hungary: namely, peace and freedom.

Historical Landmarks

1st cent. A.D.	Romans build Aquincum to control Danube frontier.
5th cent.	Attila the Hun sacks Aquincum.
896	Magyar tribes permanently settle Hungary.
1000	Coronation, in Esztergom, of Stephen (István), first king of Hungary.
1222	A type of "Magyar Carta" stipulates the rights of nobles and commoners.
1241–1242	Mongols ravage Hungary after which King Béla IV sets about reviving the wrecked nation.
1456	Turkish invaders beaten by the Hungarian army led by János Hunyadi at Nánfehérvár (Belgrade).
1514	Peasant army of young intellectuals rebel against despotic rule, but are crushed.
1526	Occupation by Turks and Habsburgs following defeat at battle of Mohács.
1686	Budapest is reclaimed from Turks by allied Christian forces from the West.
1703–1711	War of independence from Habsburg rule led by Ferenc Rákóczi; Hungarians defeated.
1848–1849	Nationalist rebellion led by Sándor Petőfi put down with aid of Russian troops.
1914	Hungary enters World War I on German side.
1920	Treaty of Trianon takes away two-thirds of Hungarian territory, including Transylvania.
1944	Hungary occupied by Nazis. Three-quarters of Budapest's buildings demolished.
1948	Russia imposes communist regime.
1956	Popular uprising crushed by Soviet tanks.
1988–1990	Perestroika leads to end of communism and Hungary's first free elections in 43 years.
1991	Hungary becomes an associate member of EC.
1994	Hungary becomes member of Council of Europe.
1997	Hungary invited to be a member of NATO

WHERE TO GO

The grey-green Danube cuts straight through the heart of the city—neatly separating the ancient cobblestone streets of Buda from the late-19th-century boulevards of Pest. If you love history you'll probably head for the Buda side of the river, but if you're a keen shopper and enjoy lively nightlife, then Pest will certainly oblige.

Orientation is rarely a problem, as the majority of sights are crammed into the central areas and getting around the city is very easy. Castle Hill is made for walking, and the rest of town is efficiently served by buses, trams, trolleybuses, and underground trains.

This section follows the natural layout of the city, starting on the western bank with Buda, Obuda, and the hills, and then moves across the Danube, stopping at Margaret Island, and over to Pest on the opposite side of the river. It is perhaps best to sample Budapest piecemeal: taking a little from one side, then crossing over the river to the other, and heading back again. However, most would agree that the best place to start is the Castle Hill.

CASTLE HILL (VARHEGY)

This fascinating area is the most picturesque and peaceful spot in Budapest, giving the only clue as to how the medieval city once looked. Entire streets of beautiful old buildings are concentrated here, and almost every other house bears a *müemlék* (monument) plaque which tells of its history. As serene as it seems today, however, the district has suffered destruction upon destruction in the past, and many places have been rebuilt at least once.

The area overlooks the city from a long, narrow plateau, divided into two: the southern part, occupied by the enor-

Highlights

All museums listed below are open from 10:00 A.M. to 6:00 P.M.

Castle Hill—northern section. Medieval streets, Church of St. Mátyás, stunning views from the beautiful Fishermen's Bastion castle battlements. *Funicular railway from Clark Adam tér or Várbusz from Moszkva tér.* (See page 24)

Gellért Baths (*Gellért fürdő*). Steam baths inside a superb Art Deco building, plus a beautiful outdoor pool. *Hotel Gellért, Gellért tér.* Opens 6:30 A.M.; closes 8:00 P.M. Monday to Friday, 2:00 P.M. Saturday, 1:00 P.M. Sunday. Tel. 166-6166. (See page 38)

Buda Hills. Peace above the city with magnificent views from János-hegy and a chairlift ride (chairlift closed some Mondays). *Cog-wheel railway then "Children's Railway."* (See page 41)

Hungarian National Museum (*Magyar Nemzeti Múzeum*). Hungarian crown jewels and displays from prehistory to 1849. Natural history. Tel. 138-2122. *Kálvin tér, M3.* (See page 50)

Houses of Parliament (*Országház*). A 19th-century gem like its London equivalent, with opulent halls. Enquire at Tourinform for visiting details. *Kossuth Lajos tér, M2.* (See page 30)

Museum of Fine Arts (*Szépművészti Múzeum*). Greek, Egyptian, and Roman relics; Renaissance art; Old Masters collection; 19th-century art. Tel. 343-9759. *Hősök tere, M1.* (See page 56)

City Park (*Városliget*). Lovely grassy park area; don't miss the splendid Széchenyi Baths (opening hours as Gellért Baths) or Vajdahunyad Castle by night. *Hősök tere, M1.* (See page 58)

Applied Arts Museum (*Iparművészeti Múzeum*). "Art Nouveau-Arabian Nights" building housing Hungarian arts and crafts exhibitions. Tel. 217-5222. *Ferenc körút, M3.* (See page 61)

Szentendre. Beautiful 18th-century town with picturesque cobbled streets full of churches, museums, and art galleries. *HÉV train from Batthyány tér.* (See page 63)

Esztergom. Spiritual centre of Hungary, boasting its biggest basilica and best collection of religious art. *Bus, boat, or hydrofoil from Budapest; bus or boat from Szentendre.* (See page 67)

The Fishermen's Bastion and the Mátyás church, seen here against the sky, are two prime sites to visit.

mous Royal Palace where the original castle once stood, and the northern district of historic streets, where 14th- and 15th-century aristocrats and artisans once rubbed shoulders.

From Pest there are various ways of getting up to Castle Hill. The most popular method of ascent is aboard the 19th-century *sikló* (funicular) which starts by the end of the Chain Bridge and rises to the Royal Palace. Alternatively take the metro to Moszkva tér, climb up the steps to the road, and catch the mini *Várbusz* service which shuttles to and from Dísz tér, stopping at numerous points en route. You could simply walk up the hill using any one of several streets and staircases, but one method you cannot use is your own transport; cars are forbidden on the hill (unless you are a resident or a guest at the Hilton Hotel), thus preserving the area's historic ambience.

Historic Streets

Turning right at the funicular terminus, a short walk brings you to Dísz tér (Parade Square) which marks the start of the northern district. The **Mátyás templom** (Matthias Church) spire, towering gracefully over this historic area, is the best reference point for our tour. The church takes its name from Hungary's favourite medieval king, who married here twice in the 15th century. The Emperor Franz Joseph I was crowned king of Hungary here in 1867, to the tune of the *Coronation Mass,* composed by Liszt for the occasion.

The original church was built in the mid-13th century, converted into a mosque during the Turkish occupation, and seriously damaged during Buda's recapture in 1686. It was rebuilt in Baroque style after the return of the Christian forces, and between 1873 and 1896 it was completely reconstructed along its present Neo-Gothic lines.

The unusual multi-coloured diamond-pattern roof and geometric designs covering the inside walls date back to the 19th-century refurbishing; the motifs are therefore Hungarian and not Turkish.

Tour guides are quick to point out the **Loreto Chapel** (immediately to the left of the entrance), where a red marble statue of the Virgin takes pride of place. At the east end of the church is the entrance to the crypt and the **museum,** which holds a fine collection of medieval stone carvings, sacred relics, historic vestments, and religious paintings. The museum rambles up and down old staircases around the church, offering at one spot an excellent view down onto the nave.

Outside the front of the church in the centre of Szentháromság tér (Trinity Square) is a votive column, crowded with statues of saints and angels, which recalls a bubonic plague epidemic of the early 18th century. The survivors built the monument in gratitude for being spared. Behind the column there is a fine Neo-Gothic building that puts on temporary exhibitions and also offers accommodation. Looking across the square, towards Dísz tér, the Baroque two-storey white building with a jutting corner balcony served as the former Buda town hall from 1710 to 1873.

Behind the church is the most photographed monument in Budapest, the intriguingly-named **Halászbástya** (Fishermen's Bastion). Built onto the castle walls, at first glance this picture-book array of turrets, terraces, and arches could easily pass for authentic medieval fortifications, but they are in fact too good to be true, constructed around the turn of this century as pure ornamentation. The name refers to the fishermen who defended the ramparts here in the 18th century. Today it is a busy place, with coachloads of tourists peering through the arches for one of the city's finest views—across the Danube and over to the Houses of Parliament. At the handsome equestrian **statue** of the canonized King Istvánn, old ladies trade Transylvanian tablecloths, zithers sing sweetly, and barrel-organs grind while classical buskers fill the air with Bartók and Liszt.

The view west from Fishermen's Bastion focuses on the startling, six-storey reflective façade of the **Budapest Hilton Hotel.** The bold approach of shamelessly merging ancient and modern has integrated the 1977 Hilton Hotel with the remains of a 17th-century Jesuit college and the tower of the district's oldest church, dating from the 13th century.

Across on Hess András tér, the bas-relief of a red hedgehog at number 3 recalls the 18th century, when the building was an inn of that name. Today on the hill there's no better place for light refreshment than Ruszwurm's, a mere scone's throw away at 7 Szentháromság utca. This cosy patisserie has been resident here since 1827; its cakes compete favourably with the best the city has to offer.

Start your tour of the old streets along **Táncsics Mihály utca**. House number 7, where Beethoven stayed in 1800, is now the charming **Museum of the History of Music.** Here you'll learn to tell your clavichord from your hurdy-gurdy and that bagpipes are also an Hungarian instrument. Next door at number 9 are plaques to political heroes Mihály Táncsics and Lajos Kossuth, both imprisoned here in the 1830s and 1840s for their nationalist beliefs. Number 26 served as a synagogue from the end of the 14th century; a small museum relates to this period. The street ends at the Bécsi kapu (Vienna Gate), a reminder that the district was once fully enclosed. The grand building next to the gate with the diamond-patterned roof—echoing that of St. Mátyás— is the **National Archive** (open to the public).

Fortuna utca is a charming, much-photographed street full of pastel-painted houses and takes its name from a tavern which stood at number 4 from 1785 to 1868. Today this

Cheerfully-painted houses lining the historic streets are a frequent target for photographers.

houses the **Museum of Commerce and Catering** (Kereskedelmi és Vendéglátóipari Múzeum)—nowhere near as grand (nor as boring) as its name suggests—dealing with confectionery in one section and Hungarian trade in the late 19th and early 20th century in another. The museum curators take a genuine delight in demonstrating various exhibits: it's well worth a visit.

At Szentháromság tér turn back into **Országház utca.** Országház, which means Houses of Parliament, takes its name from the parliamentary sessions which took place in the building at number 28 between 1790 and 1807. The architectural highlights of this street, however, are the grand 15th-century mansion, now used by the Alabárdos ("halbardier") restaurant, as well as numbers 18–22, which are considered three of the finest examples of 14th- and 15th-century domestic architecture on the hill. Several other buildings on this street incorporate picturesque medieval features, at times hidden just inside the archway. Here you'll see both ancient stone *sedilia* (built-in seats for three people) and vignettes of contemporary life with an equally timeless quality, such as necklaces of paprika strung across windows and balconies to dry; people do still live here.

At the end of this street rises a large, glassless church window. It belongs to the **Church of Mary Magdalene,** reduced to knee-high remains (by the Allies) in the last days of World War II. Amazingly, its huge, rocket-like 15th-century tower survived and now houses a private art gallery. The stone window was rebuilt, but the remainder of the church was left levelled as a poignant reminder of events. An altogether more light-hearted curiosity can be seen on the corner of Országház utca and Petermann bíró utca. A "flying nun" in stone (a reference to a convent that occupied number 28 before Parliament) has apparently passed straight through the corner of the building. Miklós Melocco executed this amusing sculpture in 1977.

Uri utca, meaning gentlemen's street, is even older than Országház utca, and the details on many of its houses are equally fascinating. Yet another specialist museum crops up at number 49; the **Telephone Museum** features 110 years of telephone exchanges and technology. Budapest had the first telephone exchange.

Locals string goulash ingredients above their balconies to keep them close at hand.

At number 9 you can descend deep into the hill via a series of tunnels that were dug in medieval times as an escape route in times of siege. They were used again as air-raid shelters and an emergency hospital in 1944–1945. Here visitors can join a guided tour of the caves and tunnels, which also contain a waxwork exhibition depicting episodes of Hungarian history.

Uri utca terminates at Dísz tér, where it's best to turn and walk back along **Tárnok utca.** Among the shops and restaurants here are a number of fine buildings. The orange-and-red geometric frescoes painted on the overhanging first floor of the Aranyhordó (Golden Barrel) restaurant are the most noteworthy. Next door, number 18 was built as a merchant's house in the first half of the 15th century. Used as the **Arany Sas** (Golden Eagle) pharmacy from 1750 until 1913, it is now the most attractive of this area's small museums. Beautiful old majolica vessels are the stars of an atmospheric re-creation of the pharmacy, and there are also informative displays

on potions, practices, and alchemy in the Budapest of this era.

The final street of this district to be explored is the leafy **Tóth Arpád sétány.** This promenade, situated along the western ramparts, offers views of the Buda Hills and the huge Southern Railway Station (*Déli pályaudavar*) rather than a glorious Danube panorama. Nonetheless, this is a delightful stroll, particularly in early evening, when the locals come out to enjoy the fresh air. At the northern end, various cannon signal the entrance to the **Museum of Military History** (*Hadtörténeti Múzeum*). It's an extensive exhibition and popular with school-children, but the section dedicated to the 1956 uprising is the most memorable for older visitors.

You'll need more than one day to see everything at the Hungarian National Gallery.

☛ The Royal Palace

Now returned to its former outward splendour, the Royal Palace dominates Castle Hill's southern skyline. Construction began in the 13th century and reached its zenith in the 15th century under King Mátyás, when the palace was said to be equal in grandeur to that of any in Europe. Under the Ottoman empire, however, it was neglected, and during the siege of 1686 was destroyed. In the following two centuries the palace was rebuilt in the Neo-Baroque style. Nemesis was on hand again when the German occupation forces made this their headquarters during a final stand in 1945. Since then, the palace has been rebuilt purely to house three museums and a library. It's a huge place and can't be covered in one day. Break up your time here with sightseeing on the northern part of the hill.

If you are not already on Castle Hill, then the best approach to the Royal Palace is from the steps at the southern tip of the hill by the Semmelweis Medical Museum. The path winds up through lovely **gardens** to the rear entrance of the castle and the only surviving turreted tower, the Buzogány (mace) Tower. Steps lead up through tiny castle gardens to the entrance of the **Museum of Budapest History** (*Budapesti Történeti Múzeum*) in wing E of the Royal Palace.

More than 40 years of excavations at the palace site have produced a picture of the medieval Royal Palace of King Mátyás; it is possible to visit the ten or so rooms that have

Those Handsome Hussars

Hussar is one of the few Hungarian words that the West is familiar with; it comes from the light cavalry brigades that were formed by King Mátyás in the late 15th century. Over the centuries their style and parts of their elegant uniform, including the famous cylindrical peaked *shako* hat, were copied by cavalry units all over Europe and came to epitomize the swashbuckling image of the mounted fighting man.

If you don't get to see latter-day hussars in the flesh (they often parade on high days and holidays), there are two fine statues on Castle Hill to admire. The equestrian statue on the corner of Uri utca and Szentháromság utca represents András Hadik, commander of Buda castle in the mid-19th century, while farther south on Uri utca, the anonymous hussar on foot is a memorial to the 1848 rebellion.

33

survived from the original, now reconstructed in their former state. Make sure you see the exhibition of Gothic statues from the Royal Palace. During construction work at the start of the 15th century, the statues were thrown out in the yard, which was later filled in, and they remained there until excavated in 1974.

The southern palace courtyard includes wing F, which houses the **National Library** and its two million books. The library is open to the public and temporary exhibitions are held in the building.

Through the courtyard arch is the main Palace area. The **Museum of Recent History** in Wing A stages some interesting "everyday life" exhibitions; visitors can also enjoy views of Buda and Pest. Wings B, C, and D house the **Hungarian National Gallery** (*Magyar Nemzeti Galéria*)—a huge undertaking spanning seven centuries of Hungarian art. Don't try to see it all in one visit—there are some fine works here, but it is too much for one day. The

gallery's most popular sections are Hungarian Impressionism and 20th century works (in Wings C and D). Contemporary art lovers are advised to head straight for the **Ludwig Collection** in wing A, which includes important figures in the contemporary art world, featuring several controversial works.

Impressionists attract the most interest at the Hungarian National Gallery.

OBUDA

Historically, Obuda is the oldest quarter of Buda, centred on the site of Aquincum, the capital of the Roman province of Lower Pannonia. Nowadays it's a nightmare of Soviet town-planning, with heavy traffic constantly rumbling past on the main northern highway out of Budapest. Amid this unlikely setting, however, there are some major Roman remains to be discovered.

To begin the Roman route, take any number of city buses north to the so-called **Military Amphitheatre** (*Katonai Amfiteátrum*), thus distinguishing it from a smaller one a short distance farther north. Gladiators performed here in the second century to amuse legionnaires. Completely forgotten for centuries, the ruins were only partially restored in the 1930s. Now it's effectively a grassy piece of parkland where locals play and walk their dogs, but enough remains of the amphitheatre walls and outline to give a good idea of what it was once like.

Farther north, beneath the Flórián tér flyover on the Buda side of the Arpád Bridge, stand the ruins of **baths** built for the Roman legions. Take the walkway on the opposite side of the flyover from the baths and you will catch the incongruous sight of a dozen isolated Corinthian columns with a 1960s housing estate backdrop.

The third and most important site is that of **Aquincum,** a civil town for the artisans, merchants, priests, and other non-military staff attached to the legion. You can get here by bus, tram, or HEV train. Keep your eyes on the highway central reservation shortly before the Aquincum stop, and you will see the remains of a Roman aqueduct.

The site proper, which covers several acres, comprises the foundations of villas (including some floor mosaics), workshops, and public areas, and there is another amphitheatre ruin on the other side of the road. You will need more than a little imagination to re-enact the scene of 1,600–1,700 years ago from the knee-high rubble, but you will find help in the small museum attached to the site. Here the best of the finds are displayed here, and, at the entrance kiosk, there are guide-books in various languages. If you want to explore the Roman connection farther, enquire at Aquincum about access to the Hercules Villa museum at Meggyfa utca 21.

But there is more to Obuda than its Roman heritage. Between Flórián tér and the river is **Főtér,** a small, picturesque cobbled square untouched by modern development. In this oasis you will find a fine old theatre, several pleasant cafés, four first-class restaurants, and, just off the square, two excellent small museum-galleries.

Even before you reach the **Imre Varga Museum** (at Laktanya utca 7), you'll half know what to expect because of the charming figures with umbrellas standing by the square. Varga is renowned as Hungary's greatest living sculptor; whether his materials and subject matter are conventional (as is the case with "Umbrellas") or offbeat, as many of his works are, he manages to be accessible and very likeable.

The **Vasarely Museum** on Szentlélek tér features first-class Op Art (a style that exploits optical effects, characterized by cubes and spheres in bright, eye-popping, checker-board colours) by artist Victor Vasarely, a pioneer of the movement.

BUDA RIVERSIDE AND HILLS

The stretch of riverside which is of most interest to visitors runs north from Szabadság híd (Liberty Bridge). While Castle Hill provides arguably the finest views over the Danube, there is another lookout point that also should not be missed. **Gellért-hegy** (Gellért Hill), which rises some 140 metres (430 feet) almost directly above the Danube on the Buda side, provides a marvellous panorama. It's not well served by public transport, so give your legs some exercise, starting from the southern approach by the Gellért Hotel.

Almost immediately to your right you will see an extraordinary monument in the hillside, a cave converted into a chapel. It belongs to the Order of St. Paul, the only monastic body of Hungarian origin. Continue up the slope through the pleasant landscaped gardens of the Jubileumi Park, turn right onto the main road, and you will soon reach the summit.

The **Citadel** crowning the hill was built by the Habsburgs after the Revolution of 1848 as a lookout point from which to control neighbouring Castle Hill. It saw no action, however, until the end of World War II, when the German army held out here. Since then the Citadel has been renovated and now holds a restaurant, café, and budget hotel.

Hotel Gellért stands on the Buda side of Liberty Bridge, which was opened in 1896.

A sanctuary for the weary walker: the Gellért Hotel has a stylish thermal bath and pool.

A **Liberation Monument** *(Szabadsag szobor)*, visible from all parts of the city, stands below the citadel. It was erected by the Russians in honour of their troops who fell while "liberating" Budapest from the Germans. The monument is loathed by most locals as a symbol of Soviet domination, but it has become too much of a city landmark to remove.

Down at the base of the hill, the **Gellért Hotel** is the perfect place to recover from your walk. Behind this classic 1918 white Art Nouveau structure is a swimming pool complex and the finest thermal bath in Buda. While the older family members may wish to enjoy the restorative thermal waters and float at leisure in the beautiful indoor pool, youngsters will most likely delight in the equally splendid landscaped outdoor pool.

There are some more baths *(fürdő)* with a wonderful atmosphere in which to relax just along the Buda embankment *(rakpart)* by the entrance to the Erzsébet híd (Elizabeth Bridge). The thermal pools are restricted to men, only. The entrance to the **Rudas fürdő** is rather shabby, and a knowledge of the language is definitely an advantage here, but after 400 years of serving the locals, change comes slowly. The building has been much altered over the centuries but the atmosphere in the steamy main pool, where a stone Turkish dome rises over an octagonal pool and sunbeams stream in through the star-shaped glass openings in the cupola, is magically ancient.

The medicinal theme continues a little farther north at the **Semmelweis Museum of the History of Medicine** (*Semmelweis Orvostörténeti Múzeum*). Professor Semmelweis, who was born here in 1815, discovered the cause of puerperal fever and thus became known as the "Saviour of Mothers." The museum is a lively, sometimes gruesome, trawl through old instruments and techniques, some of which appear far worse than the condition they were intended to relieve. There is also a beautifully preserved old pharmacy shop dating back to 1813.

North of the museum the embankment is relieved by arcades, terraces, Neo-Classical statues, ceremonial staircases, and gateways (not open to the public) which lead up to the Royal Palace.

Saint Gellért

Budapest's St. Gellért (or Gerard) was not a Hungarian native, but a Venetian, born around 980. He arrived in Hungary at a turbulent time, when King Stephen was converting the country to Christianity, and he found an admirer and sponsor in the king. Gellért wrote Hungary's first theological works, became a bishop, and founded a cathedral and monastery.

After the death of Stephen, however, Gellért fell out with the king's tyrannical successors. Paganism reasserted itself and when an uprising against King Peter (Stephen's lacklustre nephew) was brewing, Christianity became a scapegoat. Gellért was attacked during the revolt and, according to the chronicles, an enraged mob put him on a handcart and pushed him off the top of the hill which now bears his name and statue. Gellért was canonized in 1083.

At this point it's best to catch a bus or tram along the main road, Fő utca, which becomes a canyon of traffic noise, pollution, and exhaust fumes. Get off at the stop before Batthyány tér to admire the colourful exterior of the 1896 Neo-Gothic **Calvinist Church** which features in so many panoramas of the city.

Batthyány tér is a major square where metro, bus, tram, and suburban railway all meet. It is a bright, lively area, and offers a wonderful **view** of the Houses of Parliament directly across the river. The similarity to London's own Parliament (Big Ben aside) is quite striking, with the Danube simply substituted for the Thames.

The Vienna stagecoach terminal used to be just around the corner, and the once famous White Cross Inn, on the opposite side of the square to the river, was the fashionable venue for balls and festivities. It's still a grand old building even if its role has now diminished to that of a nightclub, renamed Casanova after the famous rake who reputedly stayed here. On the south side of the square is **Szent Anna templom** (St. Anne's Church), a fine mid-18th-century structure with Italianate influences.

Farther north along Fő utca is another excellent example of a Turkish bath. The **Király fürdő** (Király Baths) were established in the 16th century, and the authentic Turkish section has survived, complete with an octagonal pool under the largest dome. Apart from the steam bath, visitors can use the bath tubs, sauna, and several other facilities.

Turn left off Frakel Leó út (the continuation of Fő utca) at Margit híd (Margaret Bridge) and follow the signpost up the steps to another Turkish memento, the **Gül Baba türbéje** (the tomb of Gül Baba). This meticulously preserved mausoleum was built in the mid-16th century for Gül Baba, a famous dervish killed during the siege of Buda in 1541 whose funeral was attended by the Sultan. The interior, in keeping

with the Muslim tradition, is quite simple, with the tomb surrounded by carpets and a few artworks from the Turkish government. The hill on which the tomb stands, called the
Rózsadomb ("Hill of the Roses"), is one of the most exclu-
sive addresses in Budapest.

Buda Hills

The Buda Hills area is a greenbelt that lies due west of
Rózsadomb, though it stretches as far north as Obuda and as far
south as the start of the M7 highway. Choose a clear day, then
catch any one of several trams or buses which go past the **cog-
railway** terminus (just west of Moszkva tér, opposite the Hotel
Budapest). There is room on the train for mountain bikes if you
are feeling particularly active. The train passes smart residential houses on its way to the terminus and park of Sváb-hegy. A
short walk across the park (just follow the crowds) is the stop
for the **Children's Railway** (*Széchenyi-hegyi Gyermekvasút*),
thus named because it is operated almost entirely by school-
children; only the engine drivers are adults.

This is an old narrow-gauge line which traverses seeming-
ly unspoiled forests—but for the numerous walking trails—
and climbs, slowly, ever-upwards. At the first stop, Normafa,
you'll find a ski-run, but unless it's snowing stay on the train
until János-hegy. It is a 10–15 minute walk from here to the
János-hegy lookout tower, at 529 metres (1,735 feet) the
highest point in the city. If the horizon is not blurred by mist,
there's a splendid 360-degree view for mile upon mile; you
can also eat here.

On the way to the lookout tower you will have passed a
chair-lift that goes down to a camping site. The views from the
chair-lift are also spectacular, and the peace and quiet as you
soar up and down the mountainside is quite extraordinary. Remember to note that the chairlift is closed on some Mondays—

A heraldic detail on one of Budapest's many lovely, historic bridges.

check with Tourinform, or go on another day. If you would prefer a speedy return to town, catch the 158 bus (to Moszkva tér) from near the bottom of the chair-lift.

BETWEEN THE BANKS

Just as Tower Bridge is the toast of London, the Golden Gate is the pride of San Francisco, and the Brooklyn Bridge is a symbol of New York, Budapest too has its landmark river crossings.

The most venerable of these is the **Széchenyi Lánchíd,** or Chain Bridge, opened in 1849, the first span to unite Buda and Pest. Count István Széchenyi, a great innovator of his age, imported the technology and expertise of the British Industrial Revolution to help Hungary's own reform programme. The bridge was designed by an English engineer, William Tierney Clark, and its construction was supervised by a Scotsman, Adam Clark (no relation), who has a square named after him at the Buda end of the bridge. Don't miss the floodlit view of the bridge—it's one of the city's finest sights.

South of the Chain Bridge is the rather more functional-looking **Erzsébet híd** (Elizabeth Bridge), named after the consort of Franz Joseph, tragically assassinated in 1898. The bridge, opened in 1964, is of modern design and works on the suspension principle.

Southwards from Elizabeth Bridge is the **Szabadság híd** (Liberty Bridge) opened in 1896 and originally called the Franz Joseph Bridge. It's a handsome green iron structure with turul birds (see page 17) perched on a golden ball balancing on each pillar.

To the north of the Chain Bridge is **Margit híd** (Margaret Bridge), a modern replacement of the 19th-century version destroyed in World War II. Note the fine stone carvings of nymphs, resembling ship's figureheads, on the bridge piers.

Margaret Island (Margit-sziget)

The elite of the Roman empire escaped everyday cares on this leafy oasis between the two banks, and in later eras princes and plutocrats did likewise. Today wealthy tourists enjoy the thermal facilities and treatments offered at the two international-class hotels on the island. The leisure establishment of most interest to visitors is the huge outdoor **Palatinus Baths** (*Palatinus strand*) which includes thermal pools and boasts a capacity of 20,000 swimmers and sunbathers. The island is not just for tourists, however: Budapestis of all ages come here to walk, run, swim, play tennis or team games, or simply sunbathe. It's also a famous spot for courting couples.

Burning Bridges

Without exception, all of Budapest's bridges were destroyed by retreating German forces during the final months of World War II in order to hold up the advancing Russians. The destruction of the Margaret Bridge resulted in terrible personal tragedy for the inhabitants of Budapest. It seems that the explosives planted on the bridge went off ahead of plan, and hundreds of Budapestis crossing the river by tram and on foot in the afternoon rush hour were killed (no one knows the exact final death toll).

The only bridge not to be reconstructed in its previous form was the Erzsébet híd (Elizabeth Bridge), damaged beyond repair.

The island is 2 km (1½ miles) long and only a few hundred yards at the widest part. Many of its estimated population of 10,000 trees are now more than a century old, and large areas of the island are lawned and landscaped. Best of all, cars (with a few exceptions) are prohibited, thus preserving the island's peace and quiet.

Alongside a landmark water tower is a good **open-air theatre** which presents concerts, opera, and ballet performances in the summer. Nearby are the ruins of a 13th-century **Dominican Convent** that was founded by King Béla IV. Here he enrolled his 11-year-old daughter, Margit, in fulfilment of a vow he had made should he live to survive the Mongol invasion. Princess (and later saint) Margit stayed on the island for the rest of her life; it was subsequently named after her. Her burial place is marked by a marble plaque.

The other ruins close by include a **Franciscan Church** and monastery built in the 13th century. The charming little **Premonstratensian Chapel**—a 20th-century reconstruction of the original 12th-century church—is still in use today. It houses a 15th-century bell, the oldest in Hungary.

PEST

The bulk of modern Budapest lies to the east of the Danube in what was, until 1873, the autonomous city of Pest. Here is the true pulse of Budapest: large hotels, museums, government buildings, shopping streets, nightlife, and thunderously busy boulevards.

From the Romans' point of view, defending Buda (and therefore western civilization) was a real headache. All they could do was stare across the great expanse of flat badlands to the east of the river and wait for the barbarians to arrive. So in A.D. 294, they decided to build a defence on the east side to make it harder for any invaders to establish a foothold here. They called the place Contra-Aquincum; it is still at the core of the inner city of Pest.

The Inner City (Belváros)

A medieval town grew around the Roman defence-post, evolving into a long, narrow strip with the Danube to the west and defensive walls on the other sides. The so-called Kis-körút (Little Boulevard) follows the line of the old walls and encloses the district of Belváros. (Note that you won't find Kis-körút on any map—it's the aggregate of Vámház körút, Múzeum körút, Károly körút, the southern end of Bajcsy-Zsilinszky út, and József Attila utca.)

The oldest building in Pest is the **Belvárosi templom** (Inner City Parish Church). The exterior is rather unprepossessing—a sooty Baroque church, hemmed into an undignified position by the Elizabeth Bridge—but look inside and you can discern much earlier elements in the

The Houses of Parliament were built to represent the grandeur of the Austro-Hungarian Empire.

Timeless ambience lives on around the marble tables of the classic Gerbeaud café.

handsome interior. It was founded in the 12th century, and some Romanesque construction is still visible. So, too, is the influence of the Turks, who turned the church into a mosque and carved a *mihrab* (prayer niche) on the Mecca side of the chancel wall. Next to the church is all that remains of **Contra-Aquincum**—an excavated square with benches and a small display of tablets and reliefs found on the site.

The centrepiece of Pest's pedestrian zone is **Váci utca** (pronounced Vah-tsee utsa), the first place to visit for shopping in the city. Here you will find the best fashion, art, cosmetics, books, and jewellery; the biggest and the best branch of Folkart (see page 78); the Pest Színház (theatre) where Franz Liszt made his city debut as a 12-year-old pianist; various airline offices, and several international organizations.

Váci utca runs into the ever-busy, yet somehow relaxed, **Vörösmarty tér.** This is one of Pest's favourite gathering places, often lined with craft stalls and resounding to a brass band. After a browse through Luxus department store, it's probably time for coffee and cakes at **Gerbeaud,** doyen of Budapest's coffee-house scene since 1884. If the sumptuous high-ceilinged interior is a little too formal for your liking, then take a terrace seat and watch the world go by.

Stroll a few yards towards the river and you will come to yet another pleasant and lively square, Vigadó tér, which has the advantage of a riverside location with Castle Hill views. Here, too, you will find craft stalls and any number of buskers. A vibrant café-restaurant comprises one side of the square, but the dominant building is the splendid **Vigadó theatre.** The interior hall is an acoustically perfect auditorium renovated in 1980 (its predecessors having twice perished in war and revolution), but the façade has been gloriously re-stored in mid-19th-century Hungarian-Eastern style. The list of performers and conductors who have graced the Vigadó theatre is an impressive Who's Who of the past 150 years of European classical music: Liszt, Brahms, Wagner, Mahler, Bartók, Prokofiev, Casals, Björling, and von Karajan.

This is also the centre of what may be called "the Hotel Zone," with four luxury hotels within a very short distance of each other. Their architecture has done nothing for the aesthetics of the embankment viewed from the Buda side of the river, but, ironically, looking in the opposite direction, they provide some of the finest views of the city.

From Vörösmarty tér take Deák Ferenc utca into busy Deák tér. Just to the east of the pedestrianized zone (across Petőfi Sándor utca) are a number of intriguing buildings and two small museums. Next to the ordinary Lutheran Church is the **National Lutheran Museum,** which houses a valuable collection including documents, bibles, and chalices. It chronicles the story of some of the distinguished Protestants influential in the history of this predominantly Catholic country. As Deák tér is the only meeting point for all three metro lines, it's an apt place for the tiny **Metro Museum** (FAV Múzeum), located down in the pedestrian subway. Here you can see the original train that travelled on Europe's first continental underground railway in 1896—it's hardly different to those on the current Millennium line.

Almost opposite the Lutheran Museum, next to MacDonald's, is the helpful Tourinform tourist information office. The mustard building dominating the far side of the square is the Anker Palace, formerly an insurance company headquarters, and one of the very few structures to escape World War II unscathed.

Walk down Barczy utca, which runs along the back of the Lutheran Church, and, on your right, the Budapest **City Hall** fills an entire street. It was built in 1711 as a home for disabled soldiers, served for a time as an army barracks, and became the town hall in 1894. The 19th-century Neo-Classical Pest County Hall lies a little farther beyond the bend in the same street.

Just off here is Szervita tér, notable for a splendid patriotic-religious Art Nouveau mosaic fantasy. It occupies the very top of the old Turkish Banking House.

Head south along Petőfi Sándor utca; on your right is the **Párisi Udvar** (Paris Arcade), built in 1909. Inside, look up to enjoy the exotic Art Nouveau styling and glasswork; then walk round to see the stylish front of the building, where there is an IBUSZ tourist information office.

Directly across the busy road (it's best to use the underpass) are three fine churches and part of the university complex. On the corner of Ferenciek tere stands the **Franciscan Church,**

The vast covered market, with a ceiling six storeys above the door, is full of surprises.

constructed around 1758. Look at the relief on the side wall, depicting the flood of 1838 that caused massive destruction in the entire inner city. Then continue along Károlyi Mihály utca, past the yellow University Library building on your left. On the opposite corner is the **University Church** (Egyetemi templom). Built between 1725 and 1742 by the monks of the Order of St. Paul, it features splendidly rich Baroque carving. Turn into Szerb utca, where there are more university buildings. The **Serbian Church** on this quiet street dates from 1688 and has a beautiful interior.

The Little Boulevard

Despite its diminutive name, the Little Boulevard is very big on traffic; it is definitely not the place for a leisurely stroll. There are, however, three major points of interest that fall just outside the inner city side of this notional dividing line.

The most popular of these among locals is the Budapest **Market Halls** (Vásárcsarnok) at the beginning of Vámház körút by the Szabadság híd (Liberty Bridge). This vast, old-fashioned covered market is brimming with local colour and exotic smells. There is also a lively daily market at Lehel tér, north of the inner city in the Lipótváros district (take metro line 3 to the station at Lehel tér).

For visitors, the most popular Little Boulevard attraction is the **Hungarian National Museum** (*Magyar Nemzeti Múzeum*). This impressive structure, built in Neo-Classical style with Corinthian columns and a sculptured tympanum, stands back off the road in its own big garden. Inside, amid monumental architectural and ornamental details, the whole story of Hungary unfolds. On display are prehistoric remains

The Crown Jewels

The Hungarian royal regalia, which for the most part is much older than the famous British crown jewels, has had a long and turbulent history. In 1464 the crown was stolen from the country and King Mátyás had to ransom it back again. The crown and jewels were stolen again by a maid from the Citadel of Visegrád in the 16th century. In later centuries the regalia was buried in Transylvania (then part of Hungary) to keep it from the Habsburgs; at the end of World War II the Americans kept it safe from the clutches of the communists in Fort Knox until 1978, when it came out of exile. The jewels were then returned to Hungary, where they still reside, frequently admired, in the Hungarian National Museum.

The last king to wear the so-called Holy Crown associated with St. Stephen was the Habsburg monarch Károly IV, in 1916.

and ancient jewels and tools, but there's no doubt as to which is the main point of interest: just follow the crowd to the hushed room where the **royal regalia** resides.

The crown is romantically associated with St. Stephen, the great 11th-century king, but is actually of a slightly later date (the lower half is 11th century; the upper, 12th century). The beautiful gold-threaded mantle, made in 1031, is said to belong to St. Stephen. The sceptre also dates from around the 12th century. It's believed that both the 14th-century gilded orb and the 16th-century sword are replacements of the original regalia that was lost.

The exhibition downstairs, which deals with the history of the Carpathian Basin from prehistoric times right up to the Conquest of 896, has some good moments, particularly when covering the Roman period (it's worthwhile buying a copy of the English/German guide book, which costs only a few forints).

The exhibit upstairs, covering the period from 896 to 1849, is of more general interest than the previous millennium. A 17th-century Turkish tent decked out with carpets is one highlight, while other exhibits run the gamut of war and peace from suits of armour to room reconstructions. The museum also boasts a natural history section, but, compared to the riches of the rest of the collection, this is entirely optional viewing.

Back on the Little Boulevard, at the start of Dohány utca, is a striking synagogue of enormous proportions, built in a flamboyant Byzantine-Moorish style. This is the Central or **Great Synagogue,** dating from the mid-19th century, which is claimed by some sources to be the biggest in Europe, capable of holding up to 3,000 people. Visitors are allowed in (except during services) between 10:00 A.M. and 6:00 P.M. to appreciate its quiet grandeur.

An interesting and informative **Jewish Museum** within the complex includes a moving exhibition about the Hungarian Holocaust. Next door to the museum, in a courtyard of the synagogue, is a metal weeping-willow, fashioned by the artist Imre Varga (see page 36). Each leaf bears the name of a Budapest family that perished in the Holocaust. The site is deliberately chosen, being above the mass graves of Jews executed by the fascist Arrow Cross government installed by the Nazis between 1944 and 1945.

Lipótváros

Bounded by Jozséf Attila utca to the south and by Bajcsy-Zsilinszky út to the east, Lipótváros (Leopold Town) lies directly north of the inner city. Directions to find the **Basilica of St. Stephen** (*Szent István Bazilika*) aren't needed, as its 96-metre (315-foot) dome dominates the skyline. The biggest church in Budapest, built between 1851 and 1905, it is frequently full to its capacity of 8,500 people. Its exterior is in a poor state, though slowly being restored. Before seeing the interior, ascend the tower. It's a long walk to the top, but you are rewarded with Pest's highest viewpoint.

The interior of the basilica is dimly lit. There is an interesting main attraction in a reliquary in a rear chapel: the Szent Jobb ("Holy Right") is the much revered holy relic of the right hand of St. Stephen; you'll need a 20-forint piece to illuminate it.

Szabadság tér (Freedom Square), a short walk to the north, is probably Pest's finest architectural ensemble. At its centre is an obelisk dedicated to the Soviet troops who fell in the city, but the enormous, ostentatious buildings surrounding the square are what really steal the show. The superb lemon-coloured Art Nouveau building close to the obelisk is home to the American Embassy. Next door is the former Stock Exchange (now the country's TV headquarters), a showy, eclectic building with some good reliefs. The Hungarian National Bank on the opposite side of the square is the work of the same architect.

The great dome of Parliament, equal in height to that of the basilica, is clearly visible from the square. The **Houses of Parliament** (*Országház*) were built between 1885 and 1902 as a symbol of the grandeur of the Austro-Hungarian empire. Its vital statistics are impressive: 268 metres (879 feet) long, 691 rooms, and an estimated 20 km (12 miles) of staircase inside. The architect may not have had London's Houses of Parliament in mind, but whatever his intentions, the Neo-Gothic arches and turrets rarely escape comparison with those of Westminster.

Tourists are only admitted on group excursions, and only to certain parts of the building, when parliament is not in session; the visiting arrangements do vary from year to year (check with Tourinform as to the current situation). If you are admitted on a guided tour, you will probably be taken up the grandiose central stairway to a splendid 16-sided domed hall, then into the lobby, and finally into the principal debating chamber of the House. (Look out for the brass rack where deputies leave their cigars before they enter the chamber.)

Across from parliament is the mighty **Ethnographic Museum** (*Néprajzi Múzeum*), built in the same era, occupying the former location of the Supreme Court of Justice. It is worth a visit for the palatial interiors alone, but the exhibits here are also some of the most fascinating in the city. Permanent displays show the fast-disappearing world of Hungarian rural life and folklore; these are underpinned by trenchant temporary exhibitions dealing with current issues, such as the lives of Budapest's gypsies.

Expect to see more than Liszt's keyboard at his museum—it's said the building resounds with his music.

Andrássy út

The most attractive avenue in the city, modelled after the Champs-Elysées in Paris, was a bold stroke of the 1870s. Travelling straight as an arrow almost 2.4 km (1½ miles) from the inner city to the City Park, it is the site of some of the finest architecture in Budapest. The buildings that line it blend well, yet almost every one has a unique feature—a fountain, a statue, a mosaic or a frieze, columns or arches. There's a roomy, patrician feeling here, which belies the avenue's past names—from the unpronounceable Népköztársaság útja (People's Republic Avenue) to the prosaic Sugár út (Radial Road), to the hated Stalin út.

You can visit one of the typically large *fin-de-siècle* aristocratic homes right at the start of the avenue, at number 3, now home to the **Postal Museum.** There are some colourful and interesting exhibits here (particularly the correspondence between Thomas Edison and the Hungarian telecommunications pioneer Tivadar Puskás), but the real attraction is the building itself, particularly the stairway and balcony decorated with outstanding frescoes by Károly Lotz.

The **State Opera House** (*Andrássy út 22*), completed in 1884 by Miklós Ybl, is the most admired building on the avenue. Its Italianate style and restrained proportions fit in exquisitely with its surroundings. The splendidly opulent interior may be visited by guided tours, which are conducted daily at 3:00 and 4:00 P.M., subject to performances. The architecture, atmosphere, and acoustics of the State Opera House rank it among the very best in Europe.

If you prefer entertainment of a slightly less highbrow nature, then continue north for a block to the area known as "Budapest's Broadway," where you will find several theatres and nightspots.

The cultural theme continues on the pedestrianized area of Liszt Ferenc tér, where there is an excellent modern statue of Liszt conducting in caricature with flailing hands and windswept hair. At the end of this street is the **Academy of Music,** completed in 1907. This is an Art Nouveau gem, from the façade—where the statue and name of Liszt dominate—through to the lobby and interior. It is quite easy to get a look inside when there is no one playing.

Cross the busy intersection of Oktogon, and three streets north at Vörösmarty utca 35 is the **Ferenc Liszt Memorial Museum.** This is a delightful small collection of a few pianos, memorabilia, and period furnishings, set in an apartment where the composer once lived (closed Sunday and the first three weeks of August).

As Andrássy út heads farther away from town, the villas get noticeably grander and mansions in garden settings become predominant. **Kodály körönd** (Kodály crescent, named after another Hungarian composer) is a splendid ensemble, its curving façades decorated with Classical figures and inlaid motifs.

At number 103 is another charming small collection in the **Museum of East Asian Art** (*Hopp Ferenc Kelet-ázsiai Múzeum*), which rotates pieces from Ferenc Hopp's collection comprising 20,000 exotic items. A related **Museum of Chinese Art** (*Kína Múzeum*), also known as the *György Ráth Múzeum*, lies to the south of here, occupying a handsome Art Nouveau villa at Városligeti fasor 12.

Andrássy út ends in an outburst of pomp at **Heroes' Square** (*Hősök tere*), a huge open space housing the **Millenary Monument,** built on the thousandth anniversary of the Magyar conquest. Surmounting all is a 36-metre (118-foot) column supporting the figure of the Archangel Gabriel, who, according to legend, appeared in a dream of St. Stephen's and offered him Hungary's first crown. Around the pedestal, on horseback, sit Prince Arpád and the Magyar tribal chiefs, while flanking the column is a semi-circular colonnade with statues of historical figures, starting with King Stephen. In front of the statuary is the Tomb of the Unknown Soldier.

Facing each other across Heroes' Square are two large Neo-Classical structures that are almost mirror images—not surprising, as they share the same architect. Undergoing long-term renovation, the building on the left is the **Museum of Fine Arts** (*Szépművészeti Múzeum*), holding the city's most highly regarded collection, which ranges from Egyptian mummies and Greek and Roman relics (the latter collection is undergoing long-term restoration), through Renaissance works, to a collection of about 2,500 Old Masters, of which some 800 are on show at any one time. Italian, Dutch, German, and Spanish schools are all superbly represented. The latter is particularly notable, with masterpieces by El Greco, Goya, and several other famous names. There are also English, French, and Flemish rooms. The favourite room for many, however, is the 19th-century collection, including a treasure trove of French Impressionist and Post-Impressionist artists such as Cézanne, Pisarro, Monet, Gaugin, and Renoir, among others. The section on sculpture, and that on prints and drawings, features works by Leonardo da Vinci. The museum also has a coffee shop and a fine selection of art books and posters for sale. Free tours are given in English every weekday morning at 10:30 A.M.

Opposite the Museum of Fine Arts is the **Műcsarnok,** or "Palace of Art" (a modern art gallery), which mounts high-quality temporary exhibitions of the work of contemporary Hungarian and foreign artists. Re-opened in 1995 after undergoing renovations, the gallery boasts the finest art bookstore in Budapest, not to mention a beautiful exte-

With no two turrets the same, the Vajdahunyad castle conjures up fairytale fantasies.

rior, with a splendid pediment mosaic of St. Stephen in his role as patron saint of the arts. There is also a smaller sister branch in the City Park (directions are posted on the front of the *Műcsarnok*).

☛ City Park (Városliget)

Beyond the pompous formality of Heroes' Square and away from the noise and traffic of Andrássy út, the City Park is a lovely green space where Budapestis can relax, stroll, have a meal, hire a rowing boat, go to the zoo, or visit museums. The park, which covers some 101 hectares (250 acres), began to evolve in the early 19th century, though many of the present amenities were added during preparations for the Millennium festivities of 1896.

Cross the bridge over the boating lake, which doubles as an ice-skating rink in winter. The **Castle of Vajdahunyad,** behind the lake, was built as a prop for the Millenary Exhibition but proved so popular that it was rebuilt in permanent form. It reproduces in convincing detail part of the exterior of the fairytale Hunyadi castle in Transylvania. Inside the castle is the Museum of Hungarian Agriculture, housing a comprehensive collection that illustrates the history of hunting, fishing, and farming. If you want to see the castle at its best, return by night, when it is beautifully illuminated.

Within the grounds, there's a Catholic church with a splendid Romanesque portal (another reconstruction) and one of the city's favourite statues, which depicts the medieval chronicler who gave Hungary its first written records. Unfortunately, he didn't leave us his name, so his face is hidden deep inside the cowl of his monk's-style robe; he is referred to, simply, as Anonymous.

There are two more museums in the park, both towards its top right-hand corner. The **Museum of Aviation and Space**

Travel occupies part of the Petőfi Csarnok (Petőfi Hall), the city youth-centre where rock concerts often take place, while you will find the **Transport Museum** (*Közlekedési Múzeum*) on the perimeter path of the park. Both of these deal almost exclusively with Hungarian developments and are most likely to appeal to specialists or children.

The jewel in the park is the **Széchenyi Baths** complex, to the left of the road that bisects the park. This is one of the largest medicinal bath complexes in Europe; it also provides year-round, open-air swimming, at a constant 27°C (81°F), in beautiful surroundings. The buildings, constructed between 1909 and 1913 in a Baroque Art Nouveau style, are topped by a series of huge green domes. Inside the pool area the walls are ivy-clad and there is some sumptuous statuary, but even more interesting than the architecture of the baths is the bizarre sight of groups of men playing chess while immersed in warm water (their boards are supported on small jetties protruding into the pool).

Just behind the baths are the zoo and two amusement parks. The **zoo** welcomes visitors with an Art Nouveau entrance decorated with polar bears and elephants. It keeps a wide range of animals, including most children's and adults' favourite species. The animals are mostly held in traditional cages, though renovations on several pavilions are in progress. Grown-ups may like to note that next to the zoo is Gundel's restaurant, a legend in Hungarian culinary circles.

Vidám Park, next door, is an old-fashioned, funfair-style amusement park for the kids. You won't find American-style thrill rides here, just carousels, dodgem cars, a ferris wheel, and a few other low-technology sources of fun. A mini-version of the park more suited for younger children adjoins it. Next door to the amusement parks, a **circus** makes regular

Major Museums and Art Galleries

All below open from 10:00 A.M. to 6:00 P.M. (last admission around 5:30 P.M.) Tuesday to Sunday unless otherwise indicated. Entrance fees are nominal for all city attractions. Check opening hours in *Budapest Panorama*; check prices in *Where Budapest*.

Aquincum. Excavations open 9:00 A.M. to 6:00 P.M. Easter to September; 9:00 A.M. to 5:00 P.M. October. Museum of Roman remains and excavations. *HEV railway, Aquincum.* (See page 35)

Museum of Applied Arts (*Iparművészeti Múzeum*), Üllői út 33-37. A Hungarian arts and crafts history; also temporary exhibitions. *Ferenc körút, M3.* (See opposite page)

Budapest History Museum (*Budapesti Történeti Múzeum*). Wing E, Royal Palace, Castle Hill. Open Wednesday to Sunday from 10:00 A.M. to 6:00 P.M. March to October; closes 4:00 P.M. January and February; and 5:00 P.M. November and December. Story of Budapest until Conquest of 896 and the remains of King Mátyás 15th-century palace. *Funicular railway from Clark Adam tér.* (See page 33)

Christian Museum (*Keresztény Múzeum*), Berényi út 2, Esztergom. Religious art. *Boat or bus to Esztergom.* (See page 69)

Ethnographic Museum (*Néprajzi Múzeum*), Kossuth Lajos tér 12. Hungarian folklore. *Kossuth Lajos tér, M2.* (See page 53)

Fine Arts Museum (*Szépművészti Múzeum*), Hősök tere. Greek, Egyptian, Roman relics; Renaissance art; Old Masters; 19th-century art; prints, drawings. *Hősök tere, M1.* (See page 56)

Hungarian National Museum (*Magyar Nemzeti Múzeum*). Prehistory to Conquest of 896; from Conquest to 1849; natural history; Hungarian crown jewels. *Kálvin tér, M3.* (See page 50).

Hungarian National Gallery (*Magyar Nemzeti Galéria*). Wings B, C, D, Royal Palace. Seven centuries of Hungarian art to present. *Funicular railway from Clark Adam tér.* (See page 34)

Open Air Village Museum (*Szabadtéri Néprajzi Múzeum*), near Szentendre. 9:00 A.M. to 5:00 P.M. Tuesday to Sunday from April to October. Rural buildings and interiors. *HEV train to Szentendre then number 8 bus.* (See page 64) appearances throughout the year. For dates consult *Pro-gramme* magazine (see page 118).

If you want to return to downtown Pest, but feel you have walked enough for one day, take the **Millenium line metro,** which runs the whole length of Andrássy út (look for the antique yellow "Földalatti" signs). The quaint old-fashioned trains are a tourist attraction in their own right. Note that the trains run in the same direction as traffic, and you must descend to the platform from the appropriate side of the road; it is not possible to cross the lines once you are underground.

The Great Boulevard

The Great Boulevard (Nagy-körút) forms a long, sweeping arc from the Margaret Bridge to the Petőfi Bridge. It has, over the centuries, changed in name from Ferenc to József, to Erzsébet, to Teréz, and finally to Szent István; yet its character remains consistent—big and bustling. City planners approved the project and pushed it through during the landmark year of 1896, when the volume of traffic was considerably less than it is today. The buildings that line the boulevard are routinely six or more storeys high, many with ornate architectural touches.

The architectural pride of the Great Boulevard has to be the **Museum of Applied Arts** (*Iparművészeti Múzeum*), just off Ferenc körút at 33-37 Üllői út. The exterior is a splendid example of Art Nouveau, incorporating Hungarian folk art styles and using Hungarian majolica tiles. Great green cupolas, small spiky towers, a majolica lantern, and a bright green and gold roof top the ensemble. The architect of the museum, Ödön Lechner, is regarded as the greatest exponent of this native form of Art Nouveau style. The interior is, if anything, even more remarkable. The style itself may best be described as fantasy Hungarian with strong Moorish influences. Shimmering white *Arabian Nights*-type arches, balconies, and swirling staircases sweep up to a fine Art Nouveau skylight. The main hall is covered by a great expanse of glass supported by an iron frame, and ferns and potted plants around the hall create an exotic ambience.

A fascinating permanent exhibition, showing the progress of native arts and crafts techniques from the 12th century onwards, is augmented by a variety of temporary exhibitions, which are usually of a very high quality, on more specialized subjects.

A museum of an altogether more restrained nature lies just beyond Erzsébet körút, at Hársfa utca 47. The **Philatelic Museum** (*Bélyeg Múzeum*) contains every stamp issued by the country from 1871 onwards, and so provides its own miniature pictorial history of the country.

Teréz körút and Erzsébet körút have traditionally been centres of Budapest's cultural, as well as its commercial, life. At the Great Boulevard's intersection with Dohány utca is the **New York Café** (formerly known as the Hungaria). The café's Neo-Baroque Art Nouveau interior, shining with polished wood, brass, and cut glass, has been restored to its original gaudy glory—it looks the same as it did at the beginning of the 20th century. It is once again a meeting point for actors, writers, and journalists.

EXCURSIONS

The Danube Bend

Only a few miles north of Budapest, the Danube dramatically alters its easterly course for a southern tack. The prosaic name of this beautiful region is *Dunakanyar,* meaning Danube Bend. Here the river is at its most alluring, the countryside is lush and mostly unspoiled, and there are three delightful historic towns to explore.

Szentendre

Just 20 km (12 miles) from central Budapest, Szentendre is the most captivating of the Danube Bend settlements. The easiest way to reach it is by the HEV suburban railway from Batthyány tér. During summer, boats make a five-hour journey all the way from Budapest to Esztergom, stopping en route at Szentendre and Visegrád.

Pass up the modern suburbs and travel back to the 18th century in old Szentendre.

On your approach to Szentendre, don't be put off by the modern suburbs—the heart of the town remains virtually locked in the 18th century. Right at the centre is **Fő tér**, a picture-postcard cobblestone square. The iron rococo cross in the centre was erected in 1763 by the Serbian community (in gratitude for being spared by the plague) and the majestic Serbian church on the hill is the town's most prominent landmark.

Serbian refugees twice settled here in the wake of Turkish invasions: first in the late 13th century, and then again in 1690. On the latter occasion, around 8,000 Serbs brought their religion, art, architecture, trades and crafts, and commercial acumen to Szentendre. The church in the square, the Blagoveštenska Eastern Orthodox, is known as the **Greek Church** (Greek refugees also fled here), even though it, too, is Serbian. Built in the mid-18th century, its interior is a little gem, with a collection of Serb-painted icons well worth seeing.

On one side of the church, in what used to be an 18th-century schoolhouse, you will find the **Ferenczy Museum,** displaying works by the Hungarian Impressionist Károly Ferenczy and his two children. Another museum, on the opposite side of the church, confirms Szentendre's status as an important artists' colony. The **Margit Kovács Museum** is the former home and workshop of ceramicist Margit Kovács (1907–1977), unknown outside Hungary but worthy of an international audience. Inside there are attenuated sculptures of wide-eyed damsels, poignant religious icons, and "ordinary people," stooped and tragic, bearing the whole weight of Hungary's 20th-century misfortunes.

The rust-red, mid-18th-century **Serbian church** on the hill is only open for services, but in its grounds is the excellent Collection of Serbian Ecclesiastical Art, displaying precious carvings, icons, and manuscripts. The oldest church in the town lies just above here on top of the hill, affording a perfect vantage point from which to peer down into the tiny gardens and courtyards and across the town's venerable rooftops.

The Catholic parish church dates mostly from the 13th century, though parts of it go back to the 11th century. During summer and early autumn, craft and souvenir stalls congregate around here.

Opposite the church is another good local artist's collection, that of the Impressionist Béla Czóbel. You will find much more art on display in town, but don't miss the modern art in the **Barcsay Collection** (on the road out to the bus and railway station).

If you want a change from museums and galleries, a 4-km (2½-mile) trip out of town brings you to a great place for historic films, the **Hungarian Open Air Village Museum** (*Sza-*

badtéri Néprajzi Múzeum), which is an offshoot of the Ethnographical Museum. Catch the number 8 bus departing from the terminal next to the HEV station, and ask for the "Skanzen." There are also regular buses from the Tourinform office, on the road from the bus station to the centre.

The Visegrád area offers lookouts like this one over the beauty of the Danube.

The 46-hectare (115-acre) museum site will eventually contain ten "villages" of real houses, churches, mills, farm buildings, workshops, and smithys, dating mostly from the late 18th to the early 20th century, and culled from all over Hungary. At present there are only three settlements to view, but even these will occupy you for at least half a day and possibly longer. It is a fascinating and picturesque simulation of old rural Hungary, brought to life by active craftspeople, gingerbread makers, and other "rural folk." (Try to come on the first or third Sunday of the month, when there are several different craft demonstrations.) An excellent guide book giving the general history of the villages and buildings, and details about individual interiors, is available for purchase.

Don't miss climbing up the hill to visit the **Greek Catholic Church** from Mándok (in northeast Hungary), originally built in 1670, and boasting a painted iconostasis. The village is closed from November to April.

Visegrád

Farther up the river, where the Danube bends, lies Visegrád. You can get here by boat or the bus from Szentendre.

This is one of the most picturesque sections of the river, where verdant hillsides roll down almost to the water's edge. The finest place to enjoy the **views**—reminiscent of the best of the Rhine—are at the Citadel, high on a hill above the ruins of the old palace of Visegrád (which means "high castle" in Slavic).

The strategic value of a site commanding the river bend has been recognized since the fourth century, when the Romans built a fort here. In the 14th century, the Angevin kings of Hungary built a **palace** on the site, each monarch adding new rooms and more opulence until the establishment covered an area now estimated at some 18 hectares (44 acres). By the end of the 15th century, when King Mátyás (see page 16) was resident, the palace, like his grand Buda residence, was famous all over Europe. One rather unwilling and notorious resident was the monstrous Vlad the Impaler (on whom the Dracula legend was partly based), held prisoner here from 1462 to 1475.

Like King Mátyás's Royal Palace in Buda, the palace of Visegrád fell into ruins in the Turkish occupation and was completely forgotten. Excavations began in 1930; part of the main

A place with a view: there is more to see in Visegrád than just ancient fortifications.

building has been unearthed and certain parts have been rebuilt (using obviously new materials to differentiate these sections from the original ones). Among the best of the discoveries are the superb Hercules Fountain (a rare vestige of Hungarian Renaissance architecture), the vaulted galleries of the Court of Honour, and the restored Lion's Fountain. On the hillside, the hexagonal tower, known as the Tower of Solomon, is now a museum of the palace. Topping it all is the Citadel, which was once considered so impregnable that the Hungarian crown jewels were kept here.

The Basilica at Esztergom, the medieval capital of all Hungary, is the country's biggest church.

Esztergom

The third of the Danube Bend towns, Esztergom, situated a farther 20 km (12 miles) upriver, is linked by hydrofoil to Budapest, and by boat or bus to Szentendre and Visegrád. Take the boat if you have two hours to spare, as the river's most scenic stretch lies between Visegrád and Esztergom.

King Stephen was born in Esztergom, during his time the medieval capital of Hungary. It is still the religious centre of the country, boasting the largest church in the land. The towering **basilica** stands on the site of an 11th-century church where Stephen was crowned as the first king of Hungary in the year 1000. This church was destroyed in the struggle with the Turks, and, for all its massive dimensions (or perhaps because of its size), the only part of the current structure that generates an ancient atmosphere is the rather spooky crypt.

The most valuable part of the basilica is the red-marble side chapel called the **Bakócz-kápolna**—a pure example of Italian Renaissance style. Built in the 16th century, the chapel, taken from the ruins around it and reassembled in the 19th century, is all that survives of the original basilica. Note the white marble altar, which was sculpted by a Florentine master.

Don't miss climbing the stairs of the Basilica for two more highlights. The **treasury** contains what purports to be Hungary's richest store of religious objects, including a crystal cross from the ninth century and the 15th-century Calvary of King Mátyás. From priceless treasures, ascend the tower for a priceless **view.** As well as looking down over the town, you can also see across into Slovakia. The Danube forms a natural boundary; the bridge that up until World War I linked the two countries was symbolically left in

From Beethoven to Liszt

Construction of the Basilica of Esztergom began in 1822. Ludwig van Beethoven offered to conduct his *Missa Solemnis* for the consecration—but he died before construction was done.

During this period, however, a new, home-grown musical genius was developing. The consecration actually took place in 1856, after completion of the dome, and it was Ferenc Liszt who baptized the new basilica with his specially-conducted *Esztergom Mass* (also known as the *Gran Mass* in Germany). The basilica was eventually finished in 1869.

ruins. It's a melancholy sight that recalls Hungary's claim on that part of the land north of the river, lost in the punitive 1920 Treaty of Trianon. Those interested can cross over by ferry at this point. (Note that the treasury as well as the tower are closed from November to April.)

Alongside the basilica, the remains of a medieval royal palace have been excavated and restored, and today house the **Castle Museum.** Among the highlights in the museum are St. Stephen's Hall, the frescoed Hall of Virtues (listed as Prudence, Temperance, Fortitude, and Justice), and the 12th-century Royal Chapel.

The most popular collection in Esztergom lies at the foot of the Basilica Hill at the riverside. The **Christian Museum** (*Keresztény Múzeum*), with the most important provincial collection in Hungary, is the best religious art museum in the country. Covering mostly the Gothic and Renaissance periods from the 13th to the 16th centuries, it has some very good 14th- and 15th-century Italian paintings. Look out, as well, for the 15th-century Coffin of Garamszentbenedek, an intricately carved and painted devotional vehicle, previously paraded in the streets at Easter.

Lake Balaton

Hungary may be deprived of a coastline, but in Lake Balaton, a freshwater haven surrounded by verdant hills, fertile plains, orchards, vine-

A smiling Budapesti is a common sight, not just in the countryside but in the city, too.

yards, and historic villages, they have the next best thing. The northwest tip of Balaton is around 100 km (60 miles) from Budapest, lying within an easy and comfortable day-trip of the capital. Buses and trains serve the lake, and coach excursions visit here in summer.

Balaton is the biggest lake in central and western Europe, measuring 77 km (48 miles) across, with an area of nearly 600 km^2 (230 square miles). Yet its average depth is less than 3 metres (10 feet); in winter it freezes over completely, while in summer the shallow water is subject to wind-driven waves, and when a storm blows up even the ferries call it a day.

However, for most of the summer, the hot sun warms the tranquil lake almost up to air temperature, luring swimmers in the thousands into the water. What's more, the mildly alkaline water is said to be positively healthy for bathing—a claim that few seaside resorts can make in these days of polluted shores. The Balaton authorities also ensure that the lake is kept clean and calm by banning motor boats (with exceptions that require special permits).

Those in search of Riviera-style leisure will find a more serene equivalent around Lake Balaton.

If the fish are a barometer of a lake's health, all would appear to be hazard free: about 40 species thrive in it. Balaton pike-perch (*fogas*) is usually singled out as the tastiest of all. Fishermen operate from shore, from boats, and from platforms set a little distance into the lake. Ice-fishing has been popular since the earliest times, when winter was the only season in which the catch could be preserved and sold in distant parts of Hungary. The frozen lake is also used by ice yachtsmen, whose wind-powered boats skate at hair-raising speeds across the frozen lake.

Agriculture flourishes all along the circumference of the lake, enhancing the area with fruit trees, rippling expanses of wheat, and, in the area of Badacsony, some of the best vineyards in Hungary.

The north and south shores of the lake have their own distinct personalities. The north shore shelves quicker and, in many places, is less suited to bathing than the southern shore. The north is backed by hills, greenery, and quaint villages; the south is flatter and has extensive tourist facilities, perfect for the more hedonistic holiday-maker.

The North Shore

Driving from Budapest and navigating the lake in an counter-clockwise direction (along the perimeter Highway 71), the first settlement of any size is at **Balatonalmádi.** There is a medieval chapel in the parish church, but most people come here to enjoy the beach—the biggest and one of the best-equipped along the northern shore, with space for 12,000 sunbathing bodies. Signs for the beach read *strand,* but that won't guarantee you a sandy or even pebbly foreshore—it simply means the lake edge, which may be sand, lawn, or even concrete.

Balatonfüred, some 13 km (8 miles) farther west, has a history as a spa stretching back to Roman times. The main square, called **Gyógy tér** (meaning Health/Therapeutic Square), is a handsome place where the local mineral water bubbles up from the ground beneath a pagoda-like well-head. On three sides of the square stand grand old buildings: the 18th-century Horváth House, once an inn, now a miner's sanatorium; the Trade Union Sanatorium of 1802, and the Cardiac Hospital, which has treated heart patients from all over the world. The small grove in front of the square has a number of trees dedicated by personalities who have visited here, including Indira Gandhi.

Just off the square is Blaha Lujza utca, with a fine 1867 villa. On the opposite side of the road is the best coffee house on the lake: Kedves has been going strong for two centuries and once you've tasted their chocolate cake you'll understand why. At the end of this street is a rotund church built in the 1840s, and a small museum to the Hungarian author Mór Jókai (closed November to February). It is not all cures, coffee, and culture here: Balatonfüred is also one of the lake's liveliest resorts, bustling by day and night.

One of the most attractive spots on Lake Balaton is the village of **Tihany.** The place gives its name to a peninsula which almost cuts the lake in two and ends at the ferry point of Tihanyi-rév, where there is a Club Med-style camp and hotel offering a gamut of entertainment. The **peninsula** is unspoiled and protected by its National Park status. It even has its own small lake, popular with bird-watchers and nature lovers. To the south are the domes of former geysers.

Tihany is built high on a hill above the main lake, and its principal street, Pisky sétány (a promenade), has a few charming traditional thatched houses. Start your tour of the village below this point at the **Abbey Church** (*Apátság*), which stands just off the main road. The present 18th-century Baroque church stands over an atmospheric crypt almost a thousand years old. A rare survivor in a land constantly ravaged by so many invasions, it is claimed to be the oldest in Hungary. Here you will find the tomb of King András (Andrew) I who, in 1055, founded the Benedictine Abbey that once stood on this site. The church itself is being renovated at present, but even through the tarpaulins you can glimpse its rich Baroque carvings and decorative ornamentation.

Next door to the Abbey Church, housed in the old priory, is the **Tihany Historical Museum** (closed November to February). This museum features regional folk items and art, three small rooms where Hungary's last king, Károly IV, lived for five days in 1921, and, in the basement, an atmospheric lapidarium containing Roman remains. In front of the church, King András is commemorated in a typically offbeat Imre Varga statue, wrapped in an aluminium cloak.

Some of the quaint thatched white houses that run along Pisky sétány have been converted into an **Ethnography Museum** (similar to the one at Szentendre, see page 64, but on a much smaller scale). In the Fishermen's House, for example, you can see canoes and fishing equipment used on the lake until the 1930s (museum closed November to April).

A promenade overlooking the lake passes restaurants as well as craft and souvenir shops before it ends at Echo Hill, where the views are fine, even if the reverberations you hear aren't what they used to be. A marked path continues to the óvár—not an old castle, as the name suggests, but a volcanic outcrop dotted with cells made by monks.

The name of the region of **Badacsony** is as inextricably linked with Hungary's wine industry as that of Burgundy or Beaujolais in France. Apart from the opportunity to sample the local tipple, it's the scenery that appeals to visitors here; the region's volcanic past is evident at first sight of the conical green hills. The central basalt peak, Mount Badacsony, the biggest of all the extinct volcanoes at 437 metres (1434 feet), is invariably described as "coffin-shaped." The basalt "organ-pipes" of **Szentgyörgyhegy** are an especially fine sight. If you are feeling fit and energetic you can hike up these hills, but the easy way is by car, or by a jeep that shuttles passengers to and from the bottom of the hill to the wine museum and three small museum houses, as well as scenic points of interest.

A little way farther west, set off the main road, is the small settlement of **Szigliget.** The moody remains of a 13th-century castle offer fine views of the village and lake.

The last town on the north shore, **Keszthely** (pronounced kest-hey), was once owned entirely by the wealthy Festetics family, and their **palace** is one of Hungary's most important Baroque monuments (open all year round). Here, among a selection of its 101 rooms, you can see something of the aristocratic life the family enjoyed during the 18th and 19th centuries. The highlight is the Helikon library, claimed to be the greatest in the country, and it alone is worth the palace entrance charge (which is hefty by Hungarian standards).

A member of Hungary's dynasty, Count György Festetics, founded Europe's first agricultural school here in 1797, which is now the Keszthely University of Agricultural Sciences. A museum situated on Bercsényi utca preserves the memory of early local farming methods and equipment. The university gives the town another focus other than tourism, something unique among the lakeside settlements, and as a by-product there is a good selection of bars and restaurants.

Continuing out of Keszthely to the southwest on Highway 71, you reach another good historical collection. The **Balaton Museum** portrays the story of the settlement of the lake and the development of its people, including their agriculture and fishing and its fauna and flora, in a lively exhibition.

The South Shore

Just off the southwest corner of the lake lies **Kis-Balaton** (Little Balaton), a marshy National Reserve noted for its rare birdlife. Observation towers are provided for watchers.

Fonyód ranks as the second largest of the south shore resorts, and ferries run from here to Badacsony. A better place to

Tihany is a good starting point for exploring the eastern shores of Lake Balaton's peninsula on foot.

stay might be **Balatonföldvár,** arguably the area's most attractive resort, well-landscaped around parks and gardens.

At Szántód, the lake is squeezed to its narrowest point by the Tihany peninsula. Cars invariably queue here to make the ten-minute crossing to the north shore. On the other side of Highway 70, almost due south of the ferry point, is **Szántódpuszta.** Traditional life on the country's Great Plain (the *puszta*) is evoked through some 30 buildings dating from the 18th and 19th centuries, including a few farm buildings, a church, and a *csárda* (rustic restaurant). Displays of horsemanship, craftsmanship, and other rural activities are given regularly.

The largest town on the lake's south coast is **Siófok.** This fairly popular tourist spot boasts a *strand* which holds thousands of sunbathers and lively nightlife. Pleasure craft depart from the large harbour, but the most pleasant stretch of waterfront is the gardens immediately east of the port. Continuing eastwards, just before the hotel zone, is the town centre, which has a small museum.

The Future of Lake Balaton

The hoteliers and restaurateurs of the Balaton are fearful for the future, even though Lake Balaton has been a great favourite with German holiday-makers for years. It used to be actively promoted by the communists as a holiday spot for the people, and so provided a convenient meeting point for German friends and families split by the East–West divide. However, with the demise of communism, there is no need to meet here.

Another problem is that rising prices (endemic throughout Hungary) mean Balaton is no longer the inexpensive holiday it used to be, compared to other destinations. In spite of this, Hungarians will always continue to enjoy the lake, but most of them stay in cheap self-catering accommodation. As a hotel manager shrugs, "they have little money."

WHAT TO DO

Some people visit Budapest to pursue a special interest and happily spend their holiday in thermal pools amidst ancient Roman remains. For the less single-minded there is a wide range of activities; from high culture to late-night bars, and from sports to folk dancing. Some visitors, especially those who have been here before, may want to experience Budapest as a native by visiting one of the smaller steam baths used by the locals, horse riding on the *puszta* (plain), or bargaining for old Soviet memorabilia at the flea-market.

SHOPPING

Not very long ago, a fistful of dollars would have given you the freedom of most Budapest shopping streets. The end of communism, the imposition of VAT at 16 percent, and the effect of inflation have, however, brought an end to those bargain-basement days. As ever, artisans provide the bulk of the best buys, but it is worth bearing in mind that their hand-produced items can't compete with the price of the mass-produced substitutes from the Far East. If something is extremely cheap, chances are that it's a clever imitation.

Where to Shop

The former "Intourist" shops which only took HUF and had a virtual monopoly on quality souvenirs have been consigned to the same scrap heap as the statues of Stalin. You can now buy most Western goods in the city's department stores, at any number of specialist shops, and on market stalls; in fact, at all the usual retail outlets. Prices are nearly always fixed.

Any shopping foray should start on Váci utca, the most comprehensive and best quality shopping street in Budapest (see page 46). Here you will find a selection of clothes, fashion accessories, shoes, jewellery, antiques, books, music, china, glass, and much more.

If you are looking for folk items, start at the Folkart Centrum shop on Váci utca 14. This branch, the biggest and best of a small chain of nine outlets, is open every day. You will also find folk goods sold at stalls around Vörösmarty tér and Vigadó tér. The grocery store in the Open Air Village Museum at Szentendre is another good place to buy real artisan products.

The complimentary monthly magazines, *Where Budapest* and *Budapest Panorama,* feature shop listings. Ask Tourinform for details of the city's markets and about the Ferencváros flea-market.

What to Buy

Ceramics. The two leading brands are Herend, which is made in the town of the same name near Lake Balaton, and Zsolnay, made in the south of Hungary. The Herend factory has been turning out porcelain for the tables of the nobility since 1826; members of the British royal family from Queen Victoria to Charles and Diana have been customers. As everything is still hand-finished, prices are understandably high. You don't need to travel all the way to Herend to buy Herend ceramics, as there is a specialist shop on József Nádor tér (behind the Gerbeaud café on Vörösmarty tér).

More affordable folk-style plates and vases are common. If you want something distinctive, look for the blue-and-white ware (on sale at Tihany) or the local charcoal-coloured work.

Chess sets. There are some beautiful gift sets available for purchase in Budapest. Pawns as footsoldiers and knights as hussars in bright 18th-century garb are but one variation.

Elixirs and novelties. They say some foreigners used to fly to Hungary just to buy bottles of the wonder cure *Béres*

Csepp; you may still find it at some pharmacies. There is another miracle cocktail for sale outside the Church of Tihany.

How about a tin containing "Communism's last breath?" You will find it on sale at Vajdahunyad Castle, the Citadel, and all good joke shops.

Classical and modern porcelain figurines, kept company by an antique doll, on show in an shop window.

Food and drink. Paprika in small gift boxes or sachets, strudels packed in sturdy cardboard boxes, salami, Hungarian wines (particularly Tokay), and liqueurs (particularly apricot brandy) are popular gifts, selling at half the price, or less, than elsewhere in Europe.

Leather goods. There is plenty of Hungarian kitsch to take home, including leather wine-bottle covers and cowboy whips from the *puszta*. More seriously, handbags, gloves, and wallets are sold at reasonable, but not bargain prices.

Russian dolls. Hardly Hungarian, but a good, solid symbol of old Eastern and Central Europe. If you buy the popular Russian leaders doll, you get a miniature history lesson to boot: hidden inside Yeltsin is Gorbachev, inside Gorbachev is Andropov, and so on. This type is quite expensive.

Soviet army memorabilia. These include fur hats, steel helmets, cap and other badges, and watches. You'll find these at most markets and alongside craft stalls.

Textiles. Embroidered and handspun blouses, tablecloths, lace, blankets, and carpets can be bought from the Folkart shops or in the country. Because they involve a high degree of hand-work, prices are often high.

Woodwork. Boxes, bowls, walking sticks, and the like carved by peasants are fairly common. Look out for the fascinating "secret boxes," sometimes sold by gypsies. These appear to be unopenable, with no locks to undo or even hinges to pry open; but press a couple of panels here, slide a couple of sections there, and you're in. Don't forget the seller's instructions.

SPORTS

For a relatively small nation, Hungary has enjoyed much Olympic and World Championship success. During the mid-1950s its football team was one of the finest in the world. For the most part, national sport was for the favoured few and pursued to promote the cause of communism. Despite this, Hungary still offers spectators and participants a busy world of sports. There may be no sea, but Lake Balaton does offer a playground for watersports' fans. Horse-riders won't be disappointed either; the Hungarians have been known for their equestrian prowess ever since the Magyars swept over the Great Plain.

Taking Part

Billiards and bowling. "Billiards," which also includes tenpin bowling, snooker, and pool, is a very popular pastime in Budapest. For a list of venues ask Tourinform or see the Sports and Leisure section in the *Budapest Sun.*

Golf. This is a newcomer to Hungary, and you will have to drive some way out of town if you want to play. The Budapest Golf Course is a 9-hole, par 36 course with driving

There is nothing more romantic than a boat ride on the beautiful Danube.

range, 35 km (22 miles) north at Kisoroszi (tel. 1170-6025). Bookings are required. The nearest 18-hole course is 200 km (120 miles) away to the west in Bükk.

Horseback riding. There are numerous good stables and horse-riding schools just outside Budapest, and riding holidays around the Balaton area and farther afield are on offer at Budapesti Equestrian Club (tel. 313-5210) and Petoreházy Club Hotel (tel. 176-5937). Ask Tourinform for details, pay a visit to the aptly-named Pegazus Tours on Fereciek tere, or see the IBUSZ brochure, *Riding in Hungary.*

Ice skating. In winter the lake in the City Park is drained and turned into an ice rink with the romantic backdrop of the Vajdahunyad Castle.

Squash. The City Squash Club situated at Márcibányi tér 13 (near Moszvka tér) hires out racquets, balls, and even shoes (tel. 325-0082).

Tennis. Hungary continues to produce some good players. There are a limited number of public courts for hire, although many hotels have courts and there are numerous clubs and facilities.

Watersports. Windsurfing and yachting are widely practised on Lake Balaton and boats and boards can be hired at the main resorts. Motor boats and jet-skis are forbidden on the lake, but there is a mechanical water-ski pull at Balatonfüred and you can jet-

The steam baths, or fürdő, are the place Budapestis go to chat and relax.

ski on the Danube near Szentendre island with Jets Sport (look for the signposts near the Hotel Party on Highway 11).

Spectating

The major event of the year is the annual Formula 1 Grand Prix meeting at the Hungaroring, about 19 km (12 miles) east of town (see page 91). Other important sports events are held at the Népstadion complex a short distance to the east of the centre.

Bathtime in Budapest

After filling your stomach with goulash and chocolate pancakes, give your body a break in the nearest steam baths (*fürdő*). There are about 30 *fürdő* in Budapest, and, although they specialize in curing all manner of ailments, most Budapestis go simply for a social soak and to unwind.

The Gellért and the Széchenyi are the grandest of all, and for non-Hungarian speakers, the most accessible. They are also mixed-sex and have splendid swimming pools attached. Once you've got the hang of what's on offer, try the other baths (the Király, Rácz, or Lukács) for the local atmosphere.

A basic three-hour session costs from 700 to 1200 forints, with other treatments extra. These will be listed on a noticeboard in the foyer, but in most cases in Hungarian only. Inside the locker room you will be given a metal disc which corresponds to any treatment you have paid for, plus a towel and a cotton thong or apron to cover up. If you go from the swimming pool to the thermal baths you will probably be allowed to leave your costume on. It's a good idea to take a (waterproof) money pouch in with you, as tipping can work wonders, making the experience even more worthwhile.

Every week the locals enjoy football and horse racing—the former is Hungary's most popular spectator sport. Two of the more popular of Budapest's first division football teams are currently Kispest-Honvéd and Ferencváros. Be aware that the latter has a thuggish minority among its supporters.

The Lóverseny tér stadium at Kerepesi út 11 is the main venue for horse racing and attracts a large audience. The flat race (*galopp*) season is in summer; meetings take place on Sundays and Thursdays. Trotting (harness-racing) meetings are held all year round on Wednesdays and Saturdays at a smaller stadium also on Kerepesi út (closer to the city centre).

Details of sporting events are printed in the foreign language listings magazines or newspapers (see page 118). The Style section of the *Budapest Sun* is particularly good.

ENTERTAINMENT

Budapest has a very active nightlife, as a glance through any of the newspaper listings sections will confirm. The city is best known for what Westerners would regard as highbrow culture—theatre, opera, ballet, and particularly classical concerts. In Budapest tickets are much more democratically priced than in the West, and there is less of a class distinction amongst the audiences.

Standard popular culture is also prevalent, ranging from a bland Parisian-style cabaret to much raunchier "girly" shows. Big-name international music and showbiz acts also regularly call in at Budapest—from Jean Michel Jarre to the Chippendales. High-rollers may like to note that Budapest is eagerly embracing casinos.

Performing Arts

Theatrical life is very active: on average, several new productions give premières in Hungary each week. The city has

The grandeur of the State Opera House is echoed in the performances that take place here.

a number of fine theatres (*színház*), of which the Vigadó is probably number one. However, except for the English-language Merlin Theatre (on Gerlóczy utca, tel. 117-9338), all plays are staged in Hungarian, thus excluding most of the foreign tourists. The language barrier is, of course, much less problematic with opera, ballet, and dance or music.

The State Opera House on Andrássy út is the finest of the city's dedicated opera venues (the Vigadó also produces opera) and connoisseurs rank it among Europe's best.

Ballet is performed at the Erkel Theatre, Köztársaság tér (which also stages opera), and at the Nemzeti Színház (National Theatre) on Hevesi Sándor tér. In August the *Budafest* is a spectacular celebration of opera and ballet in the State Opera House.

The main classical music venues are in Pest: the Academy of Music (Liszt Ferenc tér), and the Basilica and the Béla Bartók Memorial House (Csalán út 29); venues in Buda include the Matthias Church and the Museum of Music History. During the summer, open-air performances are staged under the stars on Margaret Island or before authentic ancient backdrops in castle courtyards.

Tickets are available centrally: for the concert performances go to the office at Vörösmarty tér, 1; for opera, go to Andrássy út 18. Larger hotels will also make bookings for you, or you can simply go direct to the venue box office. Tourinform also sells some concert tickets. The most comprehensive listings are given by the publication *Pesti Műsor* and *Koncert Kalendárium* (Hungarian language only). A good free publication is *Pesti Est,* available at box offices, hotels, and restaurants.

Musicals from Broadway and London's West End (like *Cats, Les Misérables,* etc.) can be enjoyed in Budapest, as long as you don't mind a little Hungarian in between the songs. Tickets are on sale at the Andrássy út booking office.

There's more than just art to experience at the National Art Gallery; choral concerts are also held.

For pop, rock, and jazz concerts the best listing is the monthly publication *Budapest Panorama* (this also gives a good round-up of bars, pubs, and clubs in the city). Go to the Music Mix shop at Váci utca 33 for tickets.

Clubs and Bars

Hungary's late-night drinking and partying scene is not much different from that in other international cities. The "Pubs" are based either on the English model or, more commonly, the German *bierstube.* There is also a variety of international bars, Continental-style cafés, and authentic Hungarian bars, though the latter are not very apparent in the main tourist areas. Look for the sign *söröző* if you are a beer drinker, and *borozó* if you prefer wine. While a *söröző* is often similar to a German *bierstube,* however, a *borozó* is rarely like a Parisian wine bar (and neither serves only beer or wine).

Live music is quite common, with jazz, suppressed as subversive in the Stalinist era, currently enjoying something of a renaissance in Budapest nightspots. Most performances are blues and dixieland, and audiences are generally young. There are also several cabaret clubs presenting floorshows with big-production numbers and scantily-clad dancers.

For visitors who prefer the excitement of the casino, Hungary has 23 gambling establishments. The place to be seen is the Hilton Hotel, which (in common with most Budapest casinos) offers French and American roulette, blackjack, poker, punto banco, baccarat and, to clear you of loose change and give you a bit of exercise, slot machines. There are many other city casinos: the Las Vegas in the Atrium Hyatt; the Gresham in the Gresham Building, Roosevelt tér; the Schönbrun casino ship by the Chain Bridge; the Orfeum in the Hotel Béke; the Vigadó on Vigadó utca; and the Várkert on the Buda embankment at the southern tip of Castle Hill. The latter is housed in a beautiful neo-Renaissance building by Miklós Ybl, designer of the Opera House. Casinos generally open from 4:00 P.M. to 3:00 or 4:00 A.M.

Films

Hungarians take their movies seriously, and Hungarian directors have come up with lastingly interesting works. But the tourist is out of luck, because the domestic product is incomprehensible even locally and most of the foreign films are dubbed into Hungarian.

Folklore

Despite a recent cultural invasion from the West, Hungary still has a very active folk-music scene; and where there is music,

---

Doing the Budapest Boogie

If you want to get into the rhythm of the city's traditional music and feel sufficiently inspired by all the history around you, then join in the Magyar folkdancing held at a number of city *táncház* (dance house) venues. No one worries about folk costume, and the crowd is young and trendy.

The *táncház* phenomenon began in the 1970s when, in a reactionary roots movement, "rock-and-rollers put down their electric guitars for goatskin bagpipes and left their conservatories to travel to Transylvania to learn from the oldest village gypsies," as one local observer put it. It's not all Transylvanian—southern Slav, Bulgarian, and Greek music are also represented.

There are several venues, including the Municipal Folklore Centre, the Belvárosi Youth Centre at Molnár utca, and the Almássy tér Leisure Centre at Almássy tér 6. See *Programme* or ask Tourinform for details.

---

dancing is never very far behind. Hungarian folk-dancing is well worth watching, and takes you through the whole gamut of courtly wedding dances to high-energy, boot-slapping "Lad's Dances" from the 18th century. As ever it's best to catch it at local festivals, where performers are there for the love of dancing or local pride, as opposed to the tourist dollar. In the same vein, look out for the real gypsy dancers who have vivacity associated with the likes of Andalucian flamenco performers.

Dressed in Sunday best: young and old wear traditional costumes with pride.

You can see Hungarian dancers—amateur or professional—most nights at the Municipal Folklore Centre at Fehérvári út 47, south of Gellért Hill. Folklore evenings are also staged at other venues; the Hungarian State Folk Ensemble gives excellent performances. Folklore evenings of a different type are also touted by some restaurants. These are generally staged for tour groups on whistle-stop visits, and while they provide an easy option, they are not representative of real Hungarian folk entertainment.

CHILDREN

The main roads of Budapest, and particularly Pest, are busy with people and traffic, and children have to be closely watched. Many other areas in the city and the surrounding region, however, are much more suitable for them.

The obvious place to go is the **City Park,** where the zoo and Vidám Park are within a few yards of each other, and the circus makes regular appearances. The zoo as well as the amusement park are more traditional than modern, but the circus is reputedly one of Europe's best. If the weather is warm, the splendid **Széchenyi Baths** is the perfect place for cooling off. In summer there's a boating lake in the park and in winter this converts to an ice-skating rink.

The other oasis in the city is **Margaret Island.** You can spend a good hour or so riding round it *en famille* on a bicycle-carriage made for four. You can also swim here in the city's biggest baths, the Palatinus Strand. Children also seem to enjoy the open-air wave pool at the **Gellért Hotel.** Out of town, **Lake Balaton** is a good place for water babies, particularly the southern edge where the sandy shore slopes gently into warm water.

A cog-wheel railway and a small-gauge train takes you to the peaceful **Buda hills;** the latter is staffed almost entirely by children, apart from the driver (see page 41). The chairlift is a great favourite. It's a good idea to take along a picnic.

Older children with an interest in **horses** may enjoy a day at a riding school (see page 82) or one of the tour operators' organized horse shows. Details are available from IBUSZ or Tourinform.

Nightlife possibilities include folkdancing (see page 88) or a not-so-traditional laser show at the Planetarium in the Népliget to the southeast of the city centre.

For more useful ideas, look in the bookshops for *Budapest for Children* by Bob Dent. If you would like a copy before you leave home, write to: The *Budapest Sun,* 1068 Budapest, Dózsa György út 84a.

Calendar of Events

Dates of events and festivals appear in *Budapest Week* and other bulletins, and can be obtained from Tourinform and IBUSZ offices.

February. *Filmszemle:* A 10-day event during which new Hungarian films are screened at the Budapest Convention Centre.

March. *Budapest Spring Festival:* 10 days of the best in Hungarian music, theatre, dance, and art. *"Spring Days":* Historical dramas enacted at Szentendre.

May. *Book Week:* A carnival atmosphere pertains as Budapest sprouts bookstalls selling the new season's books.

June–August. *Summer concert season:* Budapest's open-air cinemas begin their screenings, and theatres stage light drama, musicals, opera, operetta, and revues.

July. *Historical Festival:* Esztergom stages musical performances on ancient instruments. *Hungarian Derby:* The most important horse race of the year.

August. The month when things happen. *Saint Stephen's Day:* (20th) Budapest celebrates with processions, a Craftsmen's Fair in the Castle District showing traditional crafts, and a spectacular firework display on Gellért Hill at 9:00 P.M. Other festivities in many provincial towns. *Budafest:* A celebration of opera and ballet in the State Opera House. *Wine harvest celebration:* A popular wine festival in Boglárlelle near Lake Balaton. *Hungarian Grand Prix:* Formula 1 cars race at the Hungaroring circuit.

September. *Budapest Wine Festival:* Vörösmarty tér is given over to wine-tasting stalls; festivities culminate in a colourful parade of folk from the wine-producing areas. *Wine harvest:* Takes place at Badacsony on Lake Balaton.

September/October. *Autumn Festival, Budapest Arts Weeks:* Five weeks of music, theatre, dance, and fine arts events at venues around the city, with renowned participants from all over the world.

November/December move indoors. Christmas is a family occasion. New Year's Eve takes on a carnival air.

EATING OUT

Hungarian food and drink is a serious business, but ask a foreigner to identify Magyar cuisine and the response is likely to be "paprika and goulash." Hungarian wines, however, are much better known—the deep red Bull's Blood and the smooth, sweet Tokay dessert wine are recognized beyond the country's borders. Much of Hungary's food and drink is big, robust, and rich, and the common thread linking it is "once tasted, not forgotten."

Until recently, restaurants were legally obliged to offer at least two low-priced set menus (*napi menü*) each day. Nowadays you'll probably have to order à la carte, but the choice is usually so wide that it will suit all budgets.

WHERE TO EAT

You won't often see the sign "restaurant" in Budapest, but if you do the eating-house usually caters for foreign tourists. The two most common names for an eatery are *étterem* and *vendéglő*. In the past the latter was more rustic and cheaper than the former, though nowadays there is little difference. Gypsy musicians often perform in both places. Other eating places you may see are a *büfé,* which offers hot and cold snacks, and a *csárda* (pronounced chard-a), a country inn complete with regional atmosphere. Other names to look out for are *söröző,* roughly translated as beer-hall, and *borozó,* wine-bar (see page 87). Despite their boozy names, these are sometimes just informal restaurants, and those attached to expensive hotels can be particularly good value. The food is usually the same, or similar, to that served in the hotel restaurant, but at a fraction of the price.

A typical Hungarian restaurant interior is quite rustic with high-backed wooden chairs, whitewashed walls, and folk art decorations. The lighting is usually bright and the waiting staff, often quite elderly, dress fairly formally. Establishments that cater to international business people and those on the tourist trail always provide an English translation of the menu, but others may only translate into German, if at all.

If you want fast food of the American variety you will have no problem finding Mc-Donald's and many other well-known chains. There is also a small Hungarian "Paprika" fast-food chain, and if you see a stall selling *lángos,* grab one; the deep-fried bread sprinkled with cheese and sour cream are delicious.

An informal meal al fresco is always a lovely way to end a long, full day in Budapest.

WHEN TO EAT

Breakfast (*reggeli*), served between 7:00 and 10:00 A.M., can be the tastiest meal of the day, depending of course on the establishment in which you choose to eat. The basic international breakfast buffet is generally served, comprising bacon, egg, sausage, cereal, fruit, yoghurt, cold meat, and cheese. Often you will find local pastries and possibly some foods you may not think of as usual breakfast fare, such as stuffed cabbage and other more hearty regional specialites; these dishes actually make a very satisfying meal.

Lunch (*ebéd*), taken between noon and 2:00 or 3:00 P.M., is the main meal of the day for the natives. Once you've experienced the quantity of the cuisine you'll understand why.

Dinner (*vacsora*) is served between 7:00 and 10:00 P.M. or later, though the Hungarians are by no means late eaters. Locals may opt for a cold plate rather than the usual main course, but the menu is no less extensive than at lunchtime.

In many restaurants, gypsy music often accompanies the evening meal, and for visitors this atmospheric and romantic backdrop is often an essential part of eating out in Hungary. If you enjoy the musicians playing for you, then it is customary to give them a tip. If you don't want their attention, avoid eye contact and discourage any advances to your table with a firm shake of the head.

Hungarian cuisine

The first Magyars cooked their food in a pot over an open fire on the Great Plain, and many of today's dishes still retain that earthy, outdoor feel. New seasonings and nuances came from the Slavic countries, Austria, Italy, and Turkey, and in the 17th century paprika was introduced—some say from Turkey, others say from America. This is a relatively mild seasoning obtained from a certain type of red pepper (the Serbian/ Hungarian for pepper is *paprika*), and should not be confused with the hotter-tasting chilli. Paprika is an important element in Magyar cooking, but it is by no means used in every dish.

Most food is cooked in lard rather than oil or butter (some restaurants cook only in goose fat). This tends to give a heavier, richer taste than many Western stomachs are accustomed to. If Magyar portions are too hefty for you, order soup and then an appetizer instead of the main course.

Starters (*előételek*). Cold goose liver (*hideg libabmáj zsírjában*) is a great Hungarian favourite, for starters or for a main course. It is classically fried, sliced, and served with its own fat. Another favourite is goose-liver paté. Pancakes *Hortobágy* style are filled with minced meat, deep-fried until crispy, and dressed with sour cream. Budapest may also be a good place to try caviar (*kaviár*). Prices vary enormously with quality, though the best is often the Caspian.

Goulash may be a visitor's obvious choice, but there's much more on the menu.

Soup (*leves*). Very popular with the locals and always on the menu, soup is the cheapest way of filling up. The well-known *Gulyásleves* (goulash soup) is the favourite: chunks of beef, potatoes, onions, tomatoes, and peppers with paprika, garlic, and caraway for added flavour. Fishermen's soup (*halászlé*) is also based on potatoes, onions, tomatoes, and paprika, with the addition of chunks of freshwater fish. It is traditionally served in a generous mini-cauldron made of stainless steel. Also popular and a meal in itself is Jókai bean soup (*Jókai bableves*) named after a famous writer. If you prefer a less hefty soup, try consommé with quail eggs (*erőleves fürjtojással*).

The most intriguing soup of all is *hideg meggyleves* (cold sour cherry soup). Topped with a frothy head of whipped

Meats, cheeses, and condiments tempt shoppers at the old Hungarian market.

cream, it's not a soup at all and elsewhere would be classed as a dessert. On a hot day try *hideg almaleves* (cold apple soup): creamy and refreshing, with a dash of cinnamon.

Meat (*húsételek*). Hungary is a nation of avid meat eaters. *Pörkölt* is the Hungarian stew that most closely approximates to the Westerner's notion of "goulash." *Maharpörkölt* is a beef stew, *borjúpörkölt* is veal stew, and so on. Veal and pork are the country's favourite meats, either fried (in Wiener Schnitzel), stewed, or stuffed with different combinations of ham, cheese, mushrooms, or asparagus. Steaks, too, are always on the menu. If *lecsó* is mentioned, the dish is accompanied with a stew of peppers, tomatoes, and onions.

Game and fowl. Game is very popular, as you might expect from the national affinity with meat and rich tastes. Wild boar (*vaddisznó*) and venison (*őz*) frequently appear on the menu, often very reasonably priced. Chicken (*csirke*) is always going cheap, and *csirke-paprikás*—chicken plus onion, green pepper, tomato, sour cream, and paprika—is something of a national dish. Goose is another Magyar favourite, prized for more than its liver. Turkey often comes stewed or in stuffed portions: Kiev-style (garlic butter) or cordon bleu-style (ham and cheese). Look out too for stag, hare, pheasant, and wild duck.

Fish (*halételek*). If you want to try the local fish, then obviously it has to be a freshwater variety, and carp (*ponty*) and *fogas* (a pike-perch from Lake Balaton) are the two most commonly found in Budapest. Even their greatest fans would admit that the taste of these is "delicate," and to real lovers of seafish they may appear somewhat bland.

Around Lake Balaton you may also be offered trout, pike, zander, sterlet, and wels. Fish simply grilled or baked is often priced per 10g or dekagram (dkg). To convert to the price for an average portion, multiply by 25.

Vegetables and pasta. Vegetarians have a lean time of it in Hungary. The classic dishes of stuffed pepper (*töltött paprika*) and stuffed cabbage (*töltött káposzta*) include pork in the filling, and very few restaurants offer specific vegetarian dishes. Vegetable accompaniments usually have to be ordered separately and can be uninspired. The same counts for side salads (served at some restaurants as a starter). "Cucumbers" are sometimes gherkins, and salads are often served with a strong dill dressing.

Some dishes are served with boiled potatoes, while most are eaten with pasta, either in ribbon noodles (*nokedli*) or more commonly in a heavy starchy dumpling (*galuska*) form, often translated as "gnocchi" on the English menu.

Sweets (*tészták*). There are two ubiquitous desserts in Budapest. One is the Gundel pancake (*Gundel palacsinta*), named after Hungary's most famous restaurateur. It is filled

The coffee-house culture is easy to adopt, not just for its atmosphere, but for the taste as well.

with nut and raisin paste, drenched in chocolate and rum sauce, and (if stated on the menu) flambéed. The equally calorific *Somlói galuska* is a heavy sponge affair with vanilla, nuts, and chocolate in an orange and rum sauce.

The Strudels (*rétes*) clearly reveal the Austrian influence, be they *almás* (apple), *túrós* (cottage cheese), *meggyes* (sour cherry) or, less commonly, *mákos* (poppy seed). For simpler tastes, there is always ice cream (*fagylalt*), cheese (*sajt*), or fruit (*gyümölcs*).

Drinks

Hungarian wines. Most of the wine made in Hungary is white, the most famous being Tokay (*Tokaji*). The volcanic soil of the Tokay region in the northeast of Hungary has produced "the wine of kings and the king of wines" ever since the Middle Ages. Tokay was a favourite tipple of Catherine the Great and Louis XIV; it inspired poetry from Voltaire and music from Schubert.

The term "Tokay" covers a wide selection of very drinkable table wines, but its sweet dessert wines are the most talked about. The *Tokaji furmint* is dry; *Tokaji szamorodni* is medium sweet; *Tokaji aszú* is full-bodied and sweet. The quality grade, from 3 to 5 *puttonyos* (points), is indicated on the bottle.

Less celebrated, but perfectly satisfying, white table wines come from the Lake Balaton region. The Badacsonyi wines are the best known and have been enjoyed for some 2,000 years. The Roman emperors (who first brought the vine to Hungary) liked Balaton wines so much that they shipped them back to Rome.

The most famous Hungarian red is the splendidly named *Egri bikavér* (Bull's Blood of Eger)—a full-bodied accompaniment to many of the game dishes. More subtle are the Pinot Noir from the same town and the fine *Villányi burgundi*.

If you are in a celebratory mood and want to try something novel, order a bottle of Russian champagne (*Szovjet*

Coffee and Cakes

There's no more stylish way to put on the calories than at one of Budapest's venerable coffee-houses (*kávéház*), where the prices are, by Western standards, bargain basement.

The Grand Old Lady of the city is Gerbeaud (see page 47) but the cosy atmosphere and quality of fare at Ruszwurm's on Castle Hill makes it a great favourite too. The New York Café (see page 62) is an architectural and cultural treasure in its own right. Other places to seek out are the old-style Café Művész (on Andrássy út, close to the opera), the modern coffee shops of the Hotels Forum, Gellért and Béke, and—out of town—the Kedves in Balatonfüred. Most stay open until around 10:00 or 11:00 P.M. (Művesz even later in the summertime) and also serve sandwiches, salads, and alcoholic drinks.

pezsgö). It is the best of the Eastern bubbly and around one-third the price of French champagne.

Other drinks. There are no recognized Hungarian aperitifs, but a *Puszta* cocktail is as good a way as any to start the evening. It's a mixture of apricot brandy, local cognac-style brandy, and sweet Tokay wine.

Hungarian beers (*sör*) go well with heavy, spicy foods; outside formal restaurant confines, it is as normal to drink beer with a meal as it is wine. Czechoslovakian, Austrian, and German beers make up a formidable roll-call of lagers; for a change from the light-coloured stuff, be daring and try the local Dréher dark (*barna*) beer. The "small" (*kis*) beer usually comes in a 0.2 litre glass (about half a pint), while a large (*nagy*) beer is double the quantity.

Finish off your evening with one of Hungary's famous fruit brandies (*pálinka*). They are fermented from the fruit and therefore have a clean, dry taste, as opposed to the sweet taste that results if the fruit is added later. The favourite is *barack* (apricot), followed by *cseresznye* (cherry), but several other flavours are available. The beverage that claims to be the country's national drink is the green herbal liqueur *Zwack Unicum.*

Coffee is a favourite drink of Budapestis, taken espresso-style: black, hot, and usually sweet, in thimble-sized cups. There used to be no alternative, but, unless you're way off the beaten track, you'll find milk available everywhere, and cappuccino is served all over Budapest and in the large towns.

Tea is more common than you might think, and a request for a pot of Earl Grey, or other familiar brands, with lemon or milk will raise no eyebrows in the city's better coffee-houses.

All the usual international kinds of soft drinks are available in Budapest, as is mineral water (*ásványvíz*), which is usually the sparkling type.

INDEX

HANDY TRAVEL TIPS

An A–Z Summary of Practical Information

A

ACCOMMODATION (See also CAMPING, YOUTH HOSTELS, and RECOMMENDED HOTELS)

Hotels in Budapest are graded from one star to five stars, and those in the higher bracket are of a good international standard. Until the previous decade, there was a shortage of good hotels in the city; while a number of excellent, if expensive, four-star establishments were built to fill that gap, there is still a dearth of good three-star hotels and few, if any, two- or one-star hotels that can be recommended.

If all the higher grade hotels are full, or beyond your budget, the best option is to stay slightly out of town in a *panzió* (bed and breakfast hotel). Most are set in the peaceful Buda Hills. Other options to consider are accommodation in private homes or a self-catering apartment. Neither of these are well developed for Western tourists within the city, but if you are feeling adventurous, contact the IBUSZ tourist information office for a list of addresses. Accommodation in private homes is, however, well established in the Lake Balaton area, as the numerous German *Zimmer frei* (room free) signs indicate.

Try to book ahead whenever possible, particularly during the peak seasons (see RECOMMENDED HOTELS). Tourinform tourist offices will help you with lists of accommodation, but only IBUSZ offices provide a booking service.

If you want to be comfortable in July or August you'll need air conditioning (standard in most four- and all five-star hotels).

I'd like a single room/double room.	**Egyágyas/Kétágyas szobát/kérek.**
with bath/with shower	**fürdőszobával/zuhanyozóval**
What's the daily rate?	**Mibe kerül naponta?**

AIRPORTS *(repülőtér)*

International flights operate mostly from Ferihegy airport, which is modern and offers most of the usual facilities. Terminal 2, which is used by Malév (the Hungarian national airline), Lufthansa, and Air

France, is the much better equipped of the two terminals. A third terminal is planned to be in operation by early 1999.

It takes about 45 minutes to get from the airport to the centre of Budapest (longer in heavy traffic). There's no need to take a taxi (those serving the airport are notoriously expensive), as a LRI shuttle bus runs from the arrivals terminals and calls at all the major hotels. Just look for the prominent "LRI Airport Minibus" sign.

Unfortunately, when it comes to picking you up from your hotel for your return flight, LRI is not so reliable. To get around this, when you call (24 hours in advance) for pick-up, ask them to come at least one hour before you really need to get to the airport (which gives you a chance to re-call if they forget you the first time around). If there are more than two people in your party, it may be as cheap to take a taxi. It should cost between 1,200 and 1,500 HUF.

Don't worry if you are not staying in one of the hotels at which the shuttle bus calls. LRI also run a bus service to Erzsébet tér in the centre of town every 30 minutes from 6am–10pm for 700 HUF.

B

BUDGETING FOR YOUR TRIP

Airport Transfer. Airport minibus 1,500–2,000 HUF, taxi to central Budapest 3,000–5,000 HUF, LRI bus to Erzsébet tér 500 HUF. You can also call a taxi company (see TRANSPORT), which is generally half the cost of an airport taxi.

Baths. Entrance ticket 100–160 HUF.

Camping. From 700 HUF per day for one person with car and tent or with a caravan.

Car hire. Daily rate in U.S. \$, including unlimited mileage, excluding 25 percent tax. Group A (e.g. VW Polo) 1–2 days \$59, 7 days \$47. Group B (e.g. VW Golf 1.4) 1–2 days \$70–80, 7 days \$60–70. Group C (e.g. VW Golf 1.6) 1–2 days \$80–90, 7 days \$65–90. CDW insurance \$12 per day.

Entertainment. Theatre, musicals, classical concerts 700–1000 HUF, Opera House up to 1,500 HUF.

Excursions and tours. Excursions and day trips run from a city tour for 4,400 HUF, Budapest by night for 12,000 HUF, and Balaton or Plains trips for 14,000 HUF.

Hotels. Price per night per double room in high season, central Budapest (note: prices quoted in HUF, though most luxury hotels quote prices in DM). 5-star hotel from 27.400–56,000; 4-star hotel 7,800–44,400; 3-star hotel 6,000–25,600; 2-star hotel or good quality *panzió* 4,100–17,600. Youth hostels 2,200–7,400.

Meals and Drinks. Three-course meal for one person, excluding wine and service, in a reasonable restaurant 1,500–2,000 HUF, tea/black coffee 60–100 HUF, cappuccino 100–150 HUF, small beer 150 HUF.

Museums. 20–100 HUF, Festetics Palace, Keszthely 250 HUF.

Nightlife. Casino $5–10 (refunded as betting chips).

Petrol. 140–150 HUF per litre.

Public transport. Single ride (any distance, unbroken journey, within city limits) on bus, tram, trolleybus, metro, or HEV suburban railway 80 HUF; 10-ride ticket 630 HUF; 20-ride ticket 1200 HUF; 1-day pass 700 HUF; 3-day pass 1400 HUF; 7-day pass 2000 HUF; funicular railway 80 HUF.

Taxis. The cheapest, Főtaxi and Volántaxi, have a 40–50 HUF flat charge, then cost 90 HUF/km. Unlicensed taxis charge much more.

C

CAMPING *(kemping)*

Camping facilities are generally good around Budapest and are graded from one to three stars depending on the room available per camper. Those in the Buda Hills are the most pleasantly situated, although the Római Camping site at Aquincum next to the Danube, which has an open-air swimming pool, is very popular. Some sites also offer accommodation in bungalows. Out of town there are various sites around Lake Balaton and the Danube Bend.

CAR RENTAL (See also DRIVING)

Arrangements and conditions for car hire are similar to those in other countries. The minimum age requirement is 21 and you must have been in possession of a valid licence for at least one year. U.S. and Canadian licenses are good with an international driving license.

Do shop around, as prices can vary dramatically, and be aware that on top of all quoted prices is a punishing 25 percent tax and CDW insurance to pay. Local agencies are usually the cheapest, but if you would like the reassurance of an international company, Tourinform (tel. 117-9800) recommends Avis (central office at Szervita tér; tel. 118-4158). Tourinform can also provide a list of car-hire firms.

There is no point hiring a car in Budapest unless you intend travelling farther afield than the city limits or the Danube Bend, both of which are well covered by public transport.

CLIMATE and CLOTHING

Budapest is icily cold in winter and swelters in sticky July and August. The best weather is from May to early June and in September. Temperatures in the Lake Balaton area are much the same as in Budapest and the Balaton season runs from Easter to early September.

The chart below shows Budapest's average daytime temperature:

	J	F	M	A	M	J	J	A	S	O	N	D
°C	-2	0	6	12	16	20	22	21	17	11	6	1
°F	29	32	42	53	61	68	72	70	63	52	42	34

Clothing. There is little formality of dress in Budapest. Evening gowns and jeans are both acceptable at the egalitarian Opera House. If you intend patronizing a casino, however, you will need to dress "smartly according to the season." Also, at certain upscale restaurants, formal attire is expected.

COMMUNICATIONS (See also TIME DIFFERENCES)

Post offices (*postahivatal*). These handle mail, telephone, telegraph, telex, and (at the larger offices) fax. Stamps (*bélyeg*) are best bought at tobacconists or where postcards are sold. Most hotels will stamp and post your mail for you. Postboxes are painted red.

Local post offices and the main post office at Petőfi utca are open from 8am–5 or 6pm Monday to Friday and from noon to 2pm on Saturday. In Budapest there are two 24-hour offices: Teréz körút 51 near Nyugati station, and Baross tér (near Keleti station).

Telephone (*telefon*), **telegrams** (*távirat*), **telex, and fax.** Yellow street phones, for local calls only, accept 10, 20, and 50 HUF coins. Red or blue phone boxes are for local, long-distance, and international calls and take only coins. Silver or gray phone boxes are for all types of calls, but accept only phone cards. Cards cost 600–700 HUF for 50 units or 1200 HUF for 120 units, and are available from post offices, some shops, and some hotels. Long distance and international calls can also be made through the telecommunications centre at the corner of Petőfi Sándor utca and Szervita tér. This is open from 8am–8pm Monday to Friday, 9am–3pm Saturday and Sunday.

Calls through your hotel may not be as outrageous as in other countries, as phone charges are quite cheap.

For directory enquiries in your own language, tel. 267-7111.

For international operator dial 09.

express (special delivery)	**expressz küldemény**
airmail	**légiposta**
I'd like a stamp for this letter/postcard please.	**Kérek egy bélyeget erre a levélre/a képeslapra.**
I'd like to send a telegram.	**Táviratot szeretnék feladni.**

COMPLAINTS (See also ETIQUETTE)

Every establishment in Hungary carries a "complaints book" (*panaszkönyv*), but problems are slowly, if ever, resolved by this means. It's much better to sort out the problem face to face. Ask the advice of Tourinform if you reach an impasse.

Budapest

CRIME (See also EMERGENCIES and POLICE)

As Western European capitals go, Budapest is a safe place. However, crime—almost unheard of in the communist days—is now com-
ing out of the woodwork. As far as the visitor is concerned, this
means pickpocketing (usually on the metro) or car theft. Take the
usual precautions and you should have nothing to fear.

Violence against tourists is very rare and most city streets are perfectly safe at all hours (the areas immediately around the main railway stations attract more than their share of low-life).

Report any theft to the local police (your hotel will help you) and
get a copy of your statement for your own insurance purposes.

Don't deal with black-market money-changers, as this is a crimi-
nal offence (see MONEY MATTERS).

CUSTOMS and ENTRY FORMALITIES

Everyone needs a valid passport to visit Hungary. Many countries
do not need a visa, but for specific visa regulations it's best to contact the Hungarian consulate in your own country. Visas can be obtained from any Hungarian diplomatic mission; this usually takes
less than 24 hours. If you aren't travelling by train, you can arrive
without a visa and be given one at the frontier or airport. Visas are
valid for visits of up to 90 days, and can be extended.

Duty-free. Restrictions on entering Hungary are as follows: 500 cigarettes **or** 100 cigars **or** 500*g* tobacco; 1*l* spirits **and** 1*l* wine **and** 5*l* beer.

On returning to your own country, restrictions are as follows: **Aus-
tralia:** 250 cigarettes **or** 250*g* tobacco; 1*l* alcohol; **Canada:** 200 cigarettes **and** 50 cigars **and** 400*g* tobacco; 1.1*l* spirits **or** wine **or** 8.5*l*
beer; **New Zealand:** 200 cigarettes **or** 50 cigars **or** 250*g* tobacco;
4.5*l* wine **or** beer **and** 1.1*l* spirits; **South Africa:** 400 cigarettes **and**
50 cigars **and** 250*g* tobacco; 2*l* wine **and** 1*l* spirits; **U.S.:** 200 cigarettes **and** 100 cigars or a "reasonable amount" of tobacco.

Currency restrictions. Visitors may be required to report an equivalent of 50,000 HUF or more in cash if the amount is taken out on
departure. Also, keep all exchange receipts; you may be asked to

show them. As for Hungarian currency, no more than 10,000 HUF may be brought in or out.

Leaving Hungary. You can only take out of Hungary enough food to be used during your travels, up to a value of 209,000 HUF—so salami lovers beware.

VAT. VAT (sales tax) of 16% is already included in the purchase price of most goods in Hungary. Foreigners buying a minimum 25,000 HUF worth of goods in one shop at one time can ask for a VAT certificate, have it stamped at the border customs post, and claim back the VAT—in theory. In practice you may have to leave and re-enter the country to get your refund and it will be in hard currency only if you paid in hard currency, but it's best to enquire first.

I have nothing to declare.   **Nincs elvámolni valóm.**

D

DRIVING (See also CAR RENTAL)

To take your car into Hungary you need a valid driving licence and car registration papers. Cars from most European countries (including Britain, Germany, and Austria) are presumed to be fully insured, so no extra documentation need be shown. Cars from countries that fall outside this "trustworthy" band (including France and Italy) must carry proof of insurance.

Driving regulations. Cars must be fitted with a nationality plate or sticker and rubber mudguards. A set of spare bulbs, a first-aid kit, and a warning triangle are also obligatory. The driver and all passengers must use seat belts (if available); children under 12 are prohibited from travelling in the front seat. Cars must use dipped headlights outside residential areas. It is against the law to lend a foreign-registered car to anyone, be it a Hungarian resident or another tourist.

Motorcycle riders and passengers must wear crash helmets and use dipped headlights at all times.

Budapest

Speed limits are 120 km/h (75 mph) on highways, 80 km/h (50 mph) on country roads, and 50 km/h (37 mph) in built-up areas. You may be fined on the spot for speeding.

In Hungary drinking and driving is totally prohibited.

Driving Conditions. Drive on the right and pass on the left, but be careful at all times. Hungary has one of the highest accident rates in Europe, and Budapest drivers are notorious for their recklessness. Central Budapest boulevards are many lanes wide and you have trams and trolley buses to contend with as well.

Hungary's expanding motorway system is well maintained and toll free. Yellow emergency telephones are spaced every 2 km (1¼ miles) along the Budapest–Balaton–Vienna M7 highway. Avoid this road on summer Sunday nights when it's at its busiest.

Fuel and oil *(benzin; olaj).* Filling stations are common along highways and main roads, but don't venture down minor roads without filling up. Stations are usually open 6am–10pm; there is 24 hour service in the populated areas. Unleaded fuel is widely available.

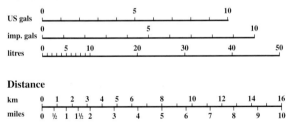

Parking. You will quickly notice that Budapest drivers have solved their on-road parking problems by transferring to the pavement. Parking is a major problem all over town, with drivers scrambling for meters and the totally inadequate number of parking-lot spaces. If you are driving, check that your hotel has parking facilities. A car parked in a prohibited zone will be towed away.

Road signs and signposts. Standard international pictographs are in use all over Hungary. Motorways are indicated by green signs, all other main roads by dark blue.

Distances. Approximate road distance in kilometers and miles between Budapest and some regional centres and border crossing points:

Balatonfüred	130 km (81 miles)	**Rábafüzes**	250 km (156 miles)
Esztergom	60 km (38 miles)	**Siófok**	105 km (66 miles)
Hegyeshalom	170 km (106 miles)	**Sopron**	210 km (131 miles)
Keszthely	155 km (97 miles)	**Visegrád**	45 km (28 miles)

Breakdowns/accidents. Remember to put out the red warning triangle 50 metres (55 yards) behind your car. All accidents must be reported within 24 hours to the Hungária Insurance Company (tel. 209-0730 x250-4; international division). If anyone is injured, the police must be notified. Cars with damaged bodywork are allowed out of the country only if they have an official certificate for the damage.

The "yellow angels" of the Hungarian Automobile Club (*Magyar Autóklub*) will come to your rescue on any major road. Just dial 088 on the roadside telephones. They do on-the-spot repairs—free for members of affiliated auto clubs—but the availability and cost of spare parts for some Western cars can be a problem. The club provides a wide range of motoring services and is based at Rómer Flóris utca 4a; tel. 212-5167 (English- and German-speaking lines).

For 24-hour breakdown service in Budapest telephone 252-8000.

Full tank, please.	**Kérem, töltse tele a tankot.**
Check the oil/tyres/battery, please.	**Kérem, ellenőrizze az olajat/a gumikat/az akkumulátort.**
I've broken down.	**Meghibásodott a kocsim.**
There's been an accident.	**Baleset történt.**
Can I park here?	**Szabad itt parkolnom?**

E

ELECTRIC CURRENT

The current is 220-volt throughout Hungary. Plugs are the standard continental type, for which British and North American appliances need an adapter.

EMBASSIES and CONSULATES *(nagykövetség; konzulátus)*

Austria: Budapest VI, Benczúr utca 16; tel. 1229-467

Canada: Budapest II, Budakeszi út 32; tel. 275-1200

Germany: Budapest XIV, Izsó utca 5; tel. 1224-204

U.K.: Budapest V, Harmincad utca 6; tel. 266-2888

U.S.: Budapest V, Szabadság tér 12; tel. 267-4400

EMERGENCIES (See also MEDICAL CARE)

Emergency telephone numbers throughout Hungary:

Ambulance	**104**
Fire	**105**
Police	**107**

24-hour medical service (English speaking) tel. 1188-212

Hungarian Automobile Club (24-hour) tel. 212-5167; Falck SOS Hungary tel. 200-0100

ENVIRONMENTAL ISSUES

You may be tempted to buy exotic souvenirs for you and your family on your holiday, but spare a thought for endangered plants and animals which could be threatened by your purchase. Even trade in tourist souvenirs can threaten the most endangered species.

Over 800 species of animals and plants are currently banned from international trade by CITES (Convention on International Trade in Endangered Species and Plants). These include many corals, shells, cacti, orchids, and hardwoods, as well as the more obvious tigers, rhinos, spotted cats, and turtles.

So think twice before you buy—it may be illegal and your souvenirs could be confiscated by Customs on your return. For further information or a factsheet contact the following:

U.K.: Department of the Environment; tel. 01179-878961 (birds, reptiles, and fish), or 01179-878168 (plants and mammals).

U.S.: Fish and Wildlife Service; tel. (703) 358-2095; fax (703) 358 2281.

ETIQUETTE (See also TIPPING)

The biggest obstacle to meeting Hungarian people is the language (see LANGUAGE) but if you do attempt a few words you'll generally get a good response. On the whole the people are friendly and helpful, if sometimes a little reserved. After so many years of living under a repressive regime, this is hardly surprising.

One possible source of confusion is how to address a Hungarian person. Firstly, the surname always precedes the Christian name; Westerners would say or write Károly Jókai, whereas Hungarians say Jókai Károly. Secondly, there is no direct equivalent of Mr. or Mrs.; the nearest terms, which are very formal, are *Uram* for Mr. and *Hölgyem* for Mrs. You can mix East and West by saying, for example, Mr. Jókai.

Good day (formal)	**Tó napot**
Hi (informal, singular/plural)	**Szia/Sziasztok**
How are you? (formal/informal)	**Hogy van/Hogy vagy?**
Very well thanks, and you? (formal/informal)	**Köszönöm, nagyon jól, és ön?/ Köszönöm, nagyon jól, és te?**

G

GAY and LESBIAN TRAVELLERS

Since the fall of communism the gay scene has mushroomed in the city to the extent that there is even a monthly gay listings magazine, *Mások* ("Outsiders"). However, as the title suggests, Budapest's gays and lesbians are not yet accepted by the mainstream community.

Budapest

Gay hangouts include the Király baths, the Palatinus baths, and the following nightspots: Mystery Bar-klub, V, Nagysándor József utca 3; Jácint Eszpresszó, V, Október 6 utca 5; Darling, V, Szép utca 1; Club 93, VIII, Vas utca 2; Angyal Bár, VIII, Szentikirályi utca 8; Lokál and "Y," VII, both on Kertész utca.

GUIDES and TOURS

There are several city and Danube Bend tours on offer through IBUSZ or other travel agencies. The most popular are the following: city introductory tour; Szentedre/Visegrád/Esztergom; Szentendre; and Danube evening cruises. Excursions farther afield visit Lake Balaton and the Great Plain for riding and folklore shows.

Walking tours and coach tours of special interest include Jewish Heritage; details from Tourinform or tel. 317-9800.

Audio-tape guides are available for hire at the National Museum and the Open Air Village Museum near Szentendre.

L

LANGUAGE

Hungarian, totally unrelated to the languages of the surrounding countries, is the mother tongue of 95 percent of the population.

By far the most widely known foreign language is German and, if you already have a smattering of this, you might do better to brush up on it, rather than attempt to learn the difficult local tongue. English is now also widely spoken and is more popular than German among younger people.

Here are a few useful phrases and some signs you are likely to see:

Yes/no	**igen/nem**
please	**kérem**
Good morning	**Jó reggelt**
Good afternoon	**Jó napot**
Good night	**Jó éjszakát**
Goodbye	**Viszontlátásra**

Thank you	**Köszönöm**
Do you speak English/French/German?	**Beszél angolul/ franciául/németül?**
entrance/exit	**bejárat/kijárat**
pull/push	**húzni/tolni**
open/closed	**nyitva/zárva**

LAUNDRY and DRY CLEANING *(mosoda; vegytisztító)*

Hotels will take care of all your cleaning problems, though often at an exorbitant price. Look up the nearest *patolyat* (an establishment offering both laundry and dry cleaning) in the Yellow Pages, if you want to save money.

When will it be ready?	**Mikor lesz kész?**
I must have this for tomorrow morning.	**Erre holnap reggelre van szükségem.**

LOST PROPERTY

Malév, Mahart (Danube shipping), railway stations, and taxi companies all have their own offices. If you lose something on the public transport system, go to Akácfa utca 18; tel. 322-6613.

For articles lost on trains go to Krisztina, krt. 37/A; tel. 322-6613. Articles found in public places are forwarded to the lost property offices of the district local authorities.

I've lost my wallet/ my handbag/my passport.	**Elvesztettem az irattárcámat/ a kézitáskámat/az útlevelemet**.

M

MEDIA

Radio. Tune into Radio Bridge (102.1 FM) for "Budapest Day and Night," an English newsmagazine transmitted at 8am and 8pm. "Voice of America News" is also broadcast on this station each hour, on the hour. Radio Budapest (61.10, 72.2, 93.85, and 1199.1 FM) broadcasts an English-language newsmagazine every night at 11pm.

Budapest

Television. There are a whole range of Hungarian TV channels, the two oldest being MTV 1 and MTV 2. MTV 1 has BBC news bulletins around midnight (times vary—see *Budapest Sun* for details) from Monday to Friday. All hotels with four or more stars (and some three-star hotels) offer satellite television and in-house videos.

Magazines. *Programme* (in English and German), *Budapest Panorama* (English/German/Italian) and *Where Budapest* (English) are the essential monthly magazines for finding out what's on. All are free and available through hotels and tourist information offices.

Young people and budget travellers should look out for *The Grapevine,* a lively bi-monthly magazine published in association with London's *Time Out* magazine.

The most comprehensive listings magazine is the weekly Hungarian-language *Pesti Műsor,* available from Tourinform.

Newspapers. The two recommended English-language weekly papers are the *Budapest Sun* and *Budapest Week,* both featuring an excellent "What's On" section. There are two other weekly English-language papers, the *Hungarian Times* and the *Hungarian Observer.* Western newspapers arrive the day after publication.

MEDICAL CARE (See also EMERGENCIES)

Many foreigners visit Budapest's therapeutic baths for health reasons, while others take advantage of the cheap dentistry available here. If you have an accident or are suddenly ill, the Hungarian National Health Service (abbreviated *Sz. T. K.*) and the emergency squad (*Mentők*) are well equipped to handle such problems. Emergency medical treatment on the scene is free; all other is payable upon receipt of service.

Ask at your hotel desk or consulate for the name of a doctor who speaks your language.

Pharmacies. Look for the sign *gyógyszertár* or *patika.* In Hungary these shops only sell pharmaceutical and related products. (For cosmetics and toiletries you'll need an *illatszerbolt* or *drogéria;* for photo supplies a *fotószaküzlet.*)

Several Budapest pharmacies stay open round the clock. Their addresses are displayed in the window of all other pharmacies. The *Budapest Sun* and Tourinform also carry a list of night pharmacies.

Where's the nearest pharmacy?	**Hol a legközelebbi patika?**
I need a doctor/dentist.	**Orvosra/Fogorvosra van szükségem.**
I have a pain here.	**Itt fáj.**
a fever	**láz**

MONEY MATTERS

Currency. The unit of currency is the *forint* (HUF) which is divided into 100 *fillér* (f). *Fillér* coins are no longer in circulation.

Coins: 1, 2, 5, 10, 20, 50, 100 HUF

Banknotes: 100, 200, 500, 1,000, 2,000, 5,000, 10,000 HUF

For import restrictions see CUSTOMS AND ENTRY FORMALITIES.

Exchange facilities. Foreign-exchange offices are found almost everywhere—in most banks, hotels, larger campsites, travel agents and large shops. Banks generally offer the best rates. Entry regulations restrict the amount of Hungarian currency that you are allowed to bring into the country, but this is hardly a problem, as there is an exchange office at the airport which stays open late. Don't forget to take your passport when you want to change money.

Don't be tempted by the numerous offers you get on the street from black-market money-changers. It is illegal to deal with them and you may well be cheated.

Keep all your exchange receipts until you leave the country.

Credit cards. Visa, Mastercard, and American Express are widely accepted, although some petrol stations take only cash.

Traveller's cheques. These may be cashed at all of the above outlets and may sometimes be substituted for cash, but you'll almost certainly get a much poorer rate of exchange than if you convert them to cash.

O

OPENING HOURS (See also PUBLIC HOLIDAYS)

Banks: 9am–2pm Monday–Friday (some close at 1pm on Friday).

Museums: 10am–6pm Tuesday–Sunday.

Offices: 8am–4pm Monday–Friday.

Post offices: 8am–6pm Monday–Friday, 8am to noon Saturday. There are two 24-hour offices (see COMMUNICATIONS).

Shops: 9 or 10am to 6 or 7pm Monday to Friday, 9 or 10am to 1 or 2pm Saturday. Some shops close all day Saturday. For 24-hour shopping look for the sign "Non-Stop."

P

PHOTOGRAPHY

There is no problem buying international brands of film in Hungary and there are quick-processing shops in Pest.

Some museums require you to buy a cheap photography permit.

I'd like some film for this camera.	**Ehhez a géphez kérnék filmet.**
black-and-white film	**fekete-fehér film**
colour prints	**színes kópiák**
colour slides	**színes diák**
35-mm	**harmincöt milliméter**
How long will it take to develop this film?	**Meddig tart előhívni ezt a filmet?**
May I take a picture?	**Lefényképezhetem?**

POLICE *(rendőrség)* (See also CRIME and EMERGENCIES)

Police wear blue-and-grey uniforms. Traffic police also wear white caps and white leather to make them more visible. During July and August Tourist police with translators also patrol the streets.

Where is the nearest police station? **Hol a legközelebbi redőrség?**

PUBLIC HOLIDAYS *(hivatalos ünnep)*

1 January	*újév*	New Year's Day
15 March	*Nemzeti ünnep*	National Holiday
1 May	*A munka ünnepe*	Labour Day
1 June	*Whitsun*	Pentecost
20 August	*Szt István ünnepe*	St. Stephen's Day
23 October	*Nemzeti ünnep*	Remembrance Day
25 December	*Karácsony első napja*	Christmas Day
26 December	*Karácsony második napja*	Boxing Day
Moveable date	*Húsvét hétfő*	(April) Easter Monday

Are you open tomorrow?   **Holnap nyitva tartanak?**

R

RELIGION

The majority of Hungarians are Roman Catholic. Mass is usually said in Hungarian, but in some churches it is in Latin, English, and German too. Other faiths, notably Protestant, Eastern Orthodox, and Jewish, are also represented.

Budapest Panorama, Where Budapest, and some English-language newspapers publish details of services in the city held in English and other languages.

T

TIME DIFFERENCES

Hungary follows Central European Time, GMT + 1. In summer the clock is put one hour ahead (GMT + 2).

Summer time:

New York	London	**Budapest**	Jo'burg	Sydney	Auckland
6am	11am	**noon**	noon	8pm	10pm

Budapest

TIPPING

Tipping is the norm in Hungary. If the service has been good you might like to give the following:

Porter, per bag	50 HUF
Maid, per week	300 HUF
Doorman, hails cab	50 HUF
Toilet attendant	50 HUF
(tip only if it is posted to do so)	
Gipsy violinist	200–300 HUF
(playing at your table)	
Masseuses in baths	100–300 HUF
Tourist guide	100–300 HUF
Theatre usher	add 20 HUF to programme sale
Filling station attendant	round up amount on pump;
	20–50 HUF for other services
Keep the change.	**A többi a magáé.**

TOILETS/RESTROOMS

Budapest is reasonably well supplied with public conveniences. Those in museums, restaurants, and coffee houses are likely to be the best bet. WC (pronounced *vay-tsay*) is a common notation, and if the pictures on the doors don't tell you which room is which, look for *férfi* (men) and *női* (women).

Where are the toilets?	**Hol a WC?**

TOURIST INFORMATION OFFICES *(turista információs iroda)*

Tourist information is dealt with by two companies, Tourinform and IBUSZ. Both have the official seal of approval.

The main Tourinform office is at Sütő utca, very close to Deák tér metro station. Staff are usually friendly and provide information on all aspects of the city. They are able to provide lists of accommodation, but cannot make bookings for you. The office is open daily from 9am–7pm. You can also telephone for information on 1179-800 or write to Tourinform, POB 215, 1364 Budapest.

The main IBUSZ office is at Sütő utca 2, 50 metres (55 yards) from the Déak tér metro station. IBUSZ is also a major tour operator and can provide a booking service and sell excursions. Opening hours are 8am to 5:30pm Monday–Friday. There is a 24-hour seven-day IBUSZ branch at Petőfi tér.

Before you leave home write to the Hungarian Tourist Board for general information:

Austria: Parkring 12, Stiege III, Stock VI, 1010 Vienna 1;
tel. (431) 512-6641, fax (431) 513-1201

France: 140 Avenue Victor Hugo, 75116 Paris;
tel. (1) 5371-6717, fax (1) 4704-8357

Germany: D-60311 Frankfurt am Main, Berliner Straße;
tel. (69) 9291 1910, fax (69) 9291 1918

U.K.: Hungarian Nat'l Tourist Board, 46 Eaton Place,
London SW1 X8AL. Information: tel. (0171) 823-1032
fax (0171) 823-1459. (Calls 39p per minute cheap rate
and 49p per minute at all other times.)

U.S.: IBUSZ, 150 East 58th Street, New York, NY 10155;
tel. (212) 355-0240, fax (212) 207-4103

TRANSPORT

The Budapest Transport Company (BKV) operates an extensive, cheap, clean, reliable system. Everywhere in central Budapest is within a few minutes' walk of a bus, tram, metro, or trolleybus line and waiting time is rarely more than a few minutes. Maps of the whole network are available from major metro and railway stations.

You can buy tickets singly, in a strip of ten, or you can save yourself the bother of having to validate them on each trip by buying a 1, 3-, 7-, or 14-day pass (you'll need a passport-sized photo for the latter two). A ticket is valid for a single unbroken ride of any distance on any service. You must buy a ticket before boarding. They are sold at all stations, travel bureaux, and tobacconists. A Budapest card entitles the holder to 3 free days of travel and discounts to museums, tours, some events, and restaurants. It is available from Tourinform offices, hotels, and main Budapest Transport Company ticket offices. The cost is 2,900 HUF.

Note that the Pioneer railway is not covered by the BKV pass, nor is the Buda Castle funicular. You will also have to pay a small fare on the HÉV to Szentendre even if you present a BKV pass, as this is only valid on the HÉV line up to the city limit.

Don't forget to validate your ticket by punching it in the red machine (passes don't need validating). These are located on board buses and trams, and for trains on line 1 of the metro. On metro lines 2 and 3 you have to use the orange machines just inside the station entrance. Few locals ever do this, as they have season tickets. You'll rarely see an inspector, but beware: they sometimes work in plain clothes. Fare dodgers have to pay an on-the-spot fine.

Most public transport runs between 4:30am and 11pm. There are a limited number of night buses and night trams (look for the suffix é on their number).

Transport within the city

Buses (*busz*). A bus stop is marked by a blue-bordered rectangular sign with the letter M (for *megálló*, meaning stop) and a list of stops on the route. Signal that you want to get off by pressing the bell.

Mini-buses. A very convenient mini *várbusz* service runs an almost constant shuttle between Moszkva tér and Dísz tér (next to the funicular railway) on Castle Hill, stopping every 200 metres.

Trolley buses (*trolibusz*). This is the service you are least likely to use, as it does not serve much of the main tourist area. It's useful for getting around the Jewish Quarter and the City Park.

Trams (*villamos*). Yellow trams, or streetcars, usually in trains of three to four carriages, cover a 190 km (120 mile) network; some run throughout the night.

Taxis (*taxi*). Budapest taxis are notorious for overcharging, and unless you're laden with luggage or háve some other reason for not travelling on public transport they are not worth the effort.

If you do want a taxi ask your hotel to call one of the following firms, which are noted for their fair prices: Főtaxi (tel. 222-2222),

Citytaxi (tel. 211-1111), Volántaxi (tel. 166-6666), Yellow Pages (tel. 155-5000).

Taxis can be hailed in the street when the "taxi" roof sign is lit, but make sure the meter is working (and at zero before you set off), or agree the fare in advance.

Underground (*földalatti or metró*). Line 1 (M1) was opened in 1896 and looks the museum piece it is—but it still does the job quite effectively. The only point where this converges with the two newer lines (M2 and M3) is at Deák tér station. Remember you have to use a new ticket each time you change lines.

River transport. Pleasure boats run to and from the Danube Bend in the summer season, departing from Vigadó tér pier. Hydrofoils also run to Esztergom and Vienna. There is no public transport service along the river.

Transport outside the city

Coaches. Coaches to the airport, other parts of Hungary, and European destinations run from the Erzsébet tér station.

Trains. There are three HÉV suburban commuter lines of which only the Batthyány tér to Szentendre (via Aquincum) service is of interest to tourists.

Inter-city trains operate from three Budapest stations: Keleti (East), Nyugati (West), and Déli (South). The latter serves Vienna.

I want a ticket to…	**Kérek egy jegyet…-ba/-be/ -ra/-rę***
single (one-way)	**egy útra**
return (round-trip)	**oda-vissza**
first/second class	**első/másod osztály**
1-day pass	**napijegy**
Will you tell me when to get off?	**Megmondaná, mikor szálljak le?**

In Hungarian prepositions are replaced by suffixes. Here you should choose one that harmonizes with the place name.

TRAVELLERS WITH DISABILITIES

Budapest is, on the whole, not well adapted for the wheelchair user and seems pretty oblivious to the situation. The tourist offices have no printed information and hardly a single gallery or museum leaflet details accessibility. The only bright spot is that the recent wave of hotel-building means an increase in accessibility; all six five-star hotels, about half of all four-star hotels and a few three- and two-star hotels claim to be accessible.

The cobbled Castle District is inherently difficult, but there is a lift at the back of the hill, by Dózsa tér. Most public transport is impossible, though the HÉV to Szentendre is manageable with a helper.

The city is equally deficient in facilities for those who are hard of hearing or visually impaired.

The following organizations may be able to answer specific enquiries from visitors with disabilities: Hungarian Society for the Rehabilitation of the Disabled, PO Box 1, H 1528 Budapest 123; National Federation of Associations of Disabled Persons, San Marco utca 76, 1032 Budapest (tel. 1888-951).

Rodata Rehabtours at Pinceszer utca 14-16, 1028 Budapest (tel. 1765-101) arrange tours and accessible accommodation for wheelchair users and other people with disabilities, using an adapted coach. Contact Katalin Zákány.

The British company Holiday Care Service are experts in the field of holidays for disabled people and will try to answer specific queries in advance of your visit; tel 0293-774535.

TRAVELLING to BUDAPEST

By air

Scheduled flights: The scheduled service operated by the Hungarian National Airline, Malév, departs daily from London to Budapest with two flights per day (flying time 2 hours 10 minutes). Scheduled flights are also available from British Airways.

Direct flights from New York (9–10 hours) now operate every day of the week.

Charter flights and package tours: Budapest is now part of every U.K. tour operator's "City Short Break" programme, sometimes combined with Vienna or perhaps Prague. As the cost of a flight (charter or scheduled) and superior accommodation in peak season are both high, you may wish to consider a package option.

Package tours from North America often include Vienna and other East European cities.

It may pay you to get a cheap flight to Vienna and then make your way onwards by train, coach, or hydrofoil.

By rail

Trains depart from London's Victoria station daily, arriving at Budapest some 28 hours later. The most direct route is via Dover to Ostend and Vienna. If money is no obstacle, catch the Venice–Simplon Orient Express at Paris, but book well in advance.

Eurotrain cards, available to students and anyone under 26, are valid for two months; they allow you to see more of East and Central Europe and are a lot cheaper than flying. Enquire, too, about a similar pass, Eastern Explorer. The Inter-rail card, available to anyone under 26 who has been a European resident, entitles you to free travel all over Europe (except Britain where the discount is about 33 percent) and is about the same price as Eurotrain.

North American citizens can get similar concessions with a Eurail pass, which must be bought at home. In the U.S. tel. (800) 4 EURAIL.

By road

The cheapest way to get from London to Budapest is by coach, which takes some 31 hours.

If you plan to drive across the Continent, the most direct route is via Ostend, Brussels, Cologne, Frankfurt, Linz, and Vienna. It's about 1730 km (1075 miles) from London.

By hydrofoil

From May to early November a hydrofoil service operates daily along the Danube to Vienna. The trip takes four to five hours one way and the price is quite reasonable.

W

WATER

Tap water is perfectly drinkable in Budapest. When visiting spa resorts you may be invited to taste waters springing from underground. Mineral water (*ásványvíz*) is usually of the sparkling variety.

WEIGHTS and MEASURES

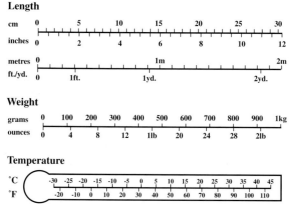

Y

YOUTH HOSTELS *(Ifjúsági szállás)*

There are about a dozen youth hostels in Budapest. You can pick up a list of addresses at Tourinform. The most central is the O&V Hostel on Papnövelde utca, by the University Church. However, the most spectacularly situated hostel accommodation is in the Citadella (see REC-OMMENDED HOTELS), which is not an official youth hostel. Contact Hungaro Hostels (tel./fax 175-2528).

Recommended Hotels

Below is a selection of hotels in different price ranges.
Hotels are graded from one star to five stars and those in
the higher bracket offer a good international standard.
Budapest has a shortage of good quality visitor accommodation, so it is always wise to book ahead, particularly for
September, New Year, Easter, and the first or second week-
end in August, when the Hungarian Grand Prix is staged.
High season on Lake Balaton is from Easter to September
and during peak times demand is such that some establishments offer only a half-board arrangement.

As a guide to room prices we have used the following
symbols to denote the price of a double room with
bath/shower in high season (normally May, June, and
early/mid August to early October) including breakfast
and tax. Note that hotel room rates are usually quoted in
Deutschmarks (DM).

✿	under 100DM
✿✿	100–180DM
✿✿✿	180–270DM
✿✿✿✿	270–360DM
✿✿✿✿+	over 360DM

BUDA—CASTLE HILL AREA

Alba ✿✿✿ *1011 Budapest, Apor Péter utca 3; Tel. 375-9244,
fax 375-9899.* Brand new hotel immediately below Castle Hill
on the river side, but set back from busy Fö utca on a quiet alley-
way. Comfortable and well appointed, with 4-star aspirations.
No restaurant. 95 rooms.

Hilton ✿✿✿✿+ *1014 Budapest, Hess Andras tér 1-3; Tel.
214-3000, fax 356-0285.* The most luxurious hotel in town, with

Budapest

arguably the best location; atop Castle Hill, with views over the Danube. This controversial ultra-modern 1976 building cleverly incorporates the remains of a Dominican church. Its restaurant is one of the best in Budapest. Business centre, *söröző*, casino. Wheelchair access. 323 rooms (suites are also available).

Kulturinnov ✿ *1014 Budapest, Szentháromság tér 6; Tel. 355-0122, fax 375-1886.* This attractive early 20th-century Neo-Gothic building is actually an "enterprise for cultural innovation and manager training." It's situated opposite the Hilton. Basic rooms but friendly staff. 18 rooms.

REST OF BUDA

Buda Penta ✿✿✿ *1013 Budapest, Krisztina körút. 41-3; Tel. 356-6333, fax 355-6964.* Plain modern building overlooking a park behind Castle Hill. Good for local public transport and next to the Southern railway station (handy for Vienna). There is a business centre, plus swimming pool, sauna, solarium, *söröző*, and nightclub. 400 rooms.

Budapest ✿✿ *1026 Budapest, Szilágyi Erzsébet fasor 47; Tel. 202-0044, fax 212-2729.* 15-storey circular block at the gateway to the Buda Hills overlooking the start of the Pioneer Railway. Panoramic views from hill-facing rooms on the upper storeys. Business centre, solarium, *borozó*, nightclub. 280 rooms; 9 suites.

Citadella ✿ *1118 Budapest, Citadella sétány; Tel. 466-5794, fax 386-0505.* Spartan but clean accommodation within the old castle. Some rooms have magnificent views. Coach invasions by day, tranquility by night (unless student groups are resident). Restaurant and *borozó*. 12 rooms.

Flamenco ✿✿✿ *1113 Budapest, Tas vezér utca 7; Tel. 372-2000, fax 372-2001.* A modern, eight-storey block opened in 1989, with a Spanish theme extending to its Bodega restaurant.

Quiet location south of Gellért Hill, slightly away from the centre, but reasonably well connected by public transport. Business centre, *borozó,* indoor pool, indoor tennis. 348 rooms.

Gellért ✪✪✪✪ *1111 Budapest, Gellért tér 1; Tel. 385-2200, fax 366-6631.* With the most character of any of Budapest's hotels, the Gellért is a city institution and its magnificent baths are a major tourist attraction. Helpful staff, excellent restaurant and coffee shop; comfortable, traditional rooms. Business centre, baths, *söröző,* and nightclub. 221 rooms, 14 suites.

Motel Vénusz ✪-✪✪ *1031 Budapest, Dózsa utca 2-4; Tel./fax 368-7252.* Simple motel rooms each with TV and telephone, all recently renovated; situated in a pleasant park on the river bank in Aquincum, 20 minutes from the city centre. Restaurant, *söröző, borozó,* swimming pool, mini-golf. 73 rooms, 4 suites.

Rubin ✪✪-✪✪✪ *1118 Budapest, Dayka Gábor utca 3; Tel. 319-3231, fax 319-3222.* Just off the busy main Vienna highway, the modern, low-rise Rubin is convenient for travellers and very well equipped. Business centre, *söröző,* bowling alley, fitness room, swimming pool, sauna, nightclub, tennis. Wheelchair access. 95 rooms.

Thermal Aquincum ✪✪✪✪ *1036 Budapest, Árpád Fejedlem útja 94; Tel. 250-3360, fax 250-4672.* A newcomer to the spa-hotel scene, the Thermal Aquincum is located by Margaret Bridge and is well placed for public transport. The decor is modern; there is a business centre and typically Hungarian *söröző.* For relaxation and entertainment there is a swimming pool and full balneotherapy facilities as well as a nightclub. Wheelchair access. 312 rooms.

BUDA HILLS

Korona Panzió ✿ *1112 Budapest, Sasadi út 127; Tel. 319-1255, fax 319-5734.* Modern chalet-style house at the foot of Sas Hill, the Korona Panzió is 10 minutes by car from the centre (also on a direct bus route). The friendly owners are accustomed to English and German guests. There is a restaurant and small garden with summer barbecue. Wheelchair access. 15 rooms.

Molnár Panzió ✿ *1124 Budapest, Fodor utca 143; Tel. 395-1873, fax 395-1872.* This modern chalet-style house enjoys a picturesque setting on the hillside known as Széchenyi mountain, 15 minutes from the city centre and within easy reach of the M7 motorway. Bedrooms are unusual and individually styled. Restaurant, bar, and pleasant outdoor terrace. 23 rooms.

Panoráma Hotel and Bungalows ✿✿ *1121 Budapest, Rege utca 21; Tel. 395-6121, fax 395-4265.* Alpine-style chalet in the Buda Hills (access via cog-railway), but only 7 km (4 miles) from Castle Hill. Bungalows also available within the hotel's 3-hectare (1.2-acre) grounds. Swimming pool, sauna, solarium, *söröző.* 35 rooms.

Petneházy Country Club ✿✿ *1029 Budapest, Adyliget Feketefej utca 2-4; Tel. 376-5992, fax 376-5738.* Perfect for sporty types, located 10 km (6 miles) from the centre of town at the foot of the Buda Hills. Comfortable wooden cabins, each with its own sauna, provide accommodation. Club facilities include swimming pool, solarium, tennis courts, and riding club. Wheelchair access. 45 cabins.

Sas Club ✿✿ *1121 Budapest, Törökbálinti út 51-53; Tel./fax 246-4643.* Stylish, modern, well-equipped chalet complex in its own grounds, 15–20 minutes from the centre and within easy access of the M7. Pleasant restaurant, *söröző,* two tennis courts, ten-pin bowling, sauna, solarium, fitness centre. 60 rooms, 13 apartments.

MARGARET ISLAND

Danubius Grand ✪✪✪✪ *1138 Budapest, Margitsziget; Tel. 329-2300, fax 329-2429.* The "Grand Old Lady" of the island, built in 1893 and renovated in 1987 without losing its palatial *fin-de-siècle* style. Business centre, swimming pool, full balneotherapy facilities, fitness room, *söröző,* wheelchair access. 162 rooms.

Thermal ✪✪✪✪ *1138 Budapest, Margitsziget; Tel. 340-4962, fax 329-3923.* Modern glass-and-concrete building with luxurious interior. Business centre, balneotherapy, fitness room, swimming pool, wheelchair access. 206 rooms.

PEST EMBANKMENT

Atrium Hyatt ✪✪✪✪-✪✪✪✪+ *1051 Budapest, Roosevelt tér 2; Tel. 266-1234, fax 266-9101.* A spectacular 10-storey glass atrium sets the tone for this stylish hotel. Rooms furnished in a contemporary but comfortable style with marvellous views across the river. Business centre, nightclub, casino, *söröző,* indoor pool, sauna, solarium, fitness room. Wheelchair access. 355 rooms.

Forum ✪✪✪✪+ *1052 Budapest, Apáczai Csere János utca 12-14; Tel. 317-8088, fax 317-9808.* This former "Amex Hotel of the Year" receives particularly high praise for the quality of its staff and its superb Silhouette restaurant. River-front rooms cost 10 percent extra. Business centre, fitness centre, indoor swimming pool, sauna, solarium. Wheelchair access. 400 rooms.

Mariott Budapest ✪✪✪✪+ *1052 Budapest, Apáczai Csere János utca 4; Tel. 266-7000, fax 266-5000.* This huge concrete building looks much better from the inside, and every luxuriously appointed room enjoys splendid views over to Castle Hill. Excellent restaurant, business centre, fitness centre, indoor swimming pool, sauna, solarium, sun-terrace, squash court. Wheelchair access. 362 rooms.

INNER CITY PEST

Astoria ✿✿✿ *1053 Budapest, Kossuth Lajos utca 19; Tel. 317-3411, fax 318-6798.* An elegant turn-of-the century atmosphere still pervades here, though the hotel was recently completely renovated. The Astoria is situated on a major traffic junction. Rooms are spacious and comfortable. Restaurant. 130 rooms, 5 suites.

Corvinus Kempinski ✿✿✿✿+ *1051 Budapest, Erzsébet tér 7-8; Tel. 266-1000, fax 266-2000.* The newest and, architecturally, the most striking of the city's many modern hotels. Very elegant bedrooms. Popular *söröző* (Pub V), business centre, indoor swimming pool, sauna, solarium, fitness centre. Wheelchair access. 367 rooms, 26 suites.

Erzsébet ✿✿✿ *1053 Budapest, Károlyi Mihály utca 11-15; Tel. 338-2111, fax 318-9237.* The Erzsébet is a well-appointed modern hotel with 4-star aspirations. It is in a central location, busy but well soundproofed. Famous *söröző*. 116 rooms, 7 suites.

Mecure Korona Hotel ✿✿✿✿ *1053 Budapest, Kecskeméti utca 14; Tel. 317-4111, fax 318-3867.* This well-equipped blue-and-pink post-modern building looks onto busy Kalvin tér, almost opposite the National Museum. Business centre, indoor pool, sauna, solarium, fitness centre. Wheelchair access. 433 rooms.

Taverna ✿✿✿ *1052 Budapest, Váci utca 20; Tel. 338-4999, fax 318-7188.* Tall, 12-storey, glass-needle-style building wedged into a narrow space on Budapest's famous shopping street. Fitness centre, sauna, solarium, ten-pin bowling, *söröző*. 224 rooms, suites.

OUTER PEST

Béke Radisson ❁❁❁❁ *1067 Budapest, Teréz körút 43; Tel. 301-1600, fax 301-1615.* Long-established hotel in a grand old building; thoroughly renovated into a luxury hotel in 1985. Handy situation for public transport links. Superb coffee shop. Business centre, casino, indoor swimming pool, solarium, sauna, fitness room. Wheelchair access. 239 rooms, 8 suites.

Grand Hotel Hungaria ❁❁❁ *1074 Budapest, Rákoczi út 90; Tel. 322-9050, fax 351-0675.* Hungary's biggest (and possibly busiest) hotel is not in one of the best areas of the city, but has so many facilities that you need rarely venture out. Pleasant rooms, good *söröző*. *Borozó,* nightclub, indoor tennis, sauna, solarium, fitness centre. 511 rooms.

Liget ❁❁-❁❁❁ *1068 Budapest, Dózsa György út 106; Tel. 269-5300, fax 269-5329.* The Liget is a post-modern-style hotel located on a busy boulevard on the edge of the City Park. Friendly staff, pleasant bedrooms. Sauna, solarium. 139 rooms.

Nemzeti ❁❁❁ *1088 Budapest, József körút 4; Tel. 269-9310, fax 314-0019.* The sky-blue façade of the once-famous National looks out cheerily onto busy Blaha Lujza tér. It was renovated in 1987 but has retained its Art Nouveau styling. Bedrooms are functional. *Söröző,* few other facilities. 76 rooms.

Thermal Helia ❁❁❁-❁❁❁❁ *1133 Budapest, Kárpát utca 62-64; Tel. 270-3277, fax 270-2262.* This new hotel enjoys a relatively relaxing location, just north of the inner city area but only a few minutes walk from a metro station. If you have the choice ask for a room with a river view. Pool and baths complex. Fitness centre, tennis court, business centre. Wheelchair access. 262 rooms.

LAKE BALATON

Annabella ❀ *Deák F. utca 25, Balatonfüred; Tel. (87) 342-222, telex (87) 343-084.* This seven-storey block hotel in Balatonfüred is surrounded by trees; close to the lakeside and main park, with its own beach. Good restaurant, *söröző*, nightclub. Facilities include swimming pool, solarium, windsurf hire. 385 rooms.

Auróra ❀ *Bajcsy-Zsilinszky utca 14, Balatonalmádi; Tel. (88) 338-810, fax (88) 338-410.* This 14-storey hotel enjoys a quiet location in a park on top of a small hill with excellent views in all directions. The lake is just a few minutes' walk away, and the hotel has its own private beach. Facilities include an indoor swimming pool, sauna, solarium, ten-pin bowling alley, tennis courts (nearby), night club. 240 rooms.

Club Tihany Bungalows Hotel ❀❀❀-❀❀❀❀ *8237 Tihany-rév, Tihany; Tel. (87) 448-088, fax (87) 448-083.* A holiday village complex near the Tihany ferry comprising a small hotel with 20 rooms, a larger hotel with 330 rooms and 24 suites (half-board only), and 161 luxury bungalows, each with kitchen. Private beach, indoor and outdoor swimming pools, sauna, solarium, ten-pin bowling, indoor and outdoor tennis courts, squash courts, horse-riding, fitness room, nightclub. Wheelchair access.

Füred ❀❀ *Széchenyi utca 20, Balatonfüred; Tel. (87) 343-033, telex (87) 343-034.* Lake-facing rooms on the upper floors of this modern 14-storey block enjoy views across to Tihany. Private lakeside sunbathing lawns and jetty with boats for hire. Ten-pin bowling alley, tennis court, *borozó*. 152 rooms.

Hullám ❀❀ *8360 Keszthely Balatonpart, Keszthely; Tel. (83) 312-644, fax (83) 315-950.* Pleasant, old wooden chalet-type hotel right on the lakeside. Friendly staff. Swimming pool, tennis court nearby, *söröző*. 50 rooms.

Recommended Restaurants

Below is a selection of some of Budapest's best restaurants in different price bands. Book ahead wherever possible for lunchtime (the main meal of the day) and dinner. Some restaurants stay open throughout the afternoon. The only time when restaurants are likely to be closed is Sunday night.

In Hungary, menu prices generally do not include service. To give you an idea of the price for an average three course meal per person, excluding wine and service, we have used the following symbols:

❀	up to 1,300 HUF
❀❀	1,300–2,200 HUF
❀❀❀	2,200–3,100 HUF
❀❀❀❀	above 3,100 HUF

BUDA—CASTLE HILL AREA

Alabárdos ❀❀❀❀ *Országház utca 2; Tel. 356-0851.* This grand old 15th-century mansion retains atmospheric furnishings and fittings and provides excellent cuisine and service. Try a flambeéd dish for maximum attention. Closed Sunday. Reservations and formal attire required.

Angelika Kávéház ❀ *Batthyány tér 7; Tel. 212-3784.* A beautiful traditional café replete with wood-paneling and mirrors, offering a large selection of Hungarian and Viennese pastries. Open daily from 10am–10pm. Credit cards not accepted.

Aranyhordó ❀❀ *Tárnok utca 16; Tel. 356-1367.* Not just a single restaurant, this is a famous old eating house including a *söröző*, a café, and a stylish restaurant, all in an attractive 14th-century building. Specialities include *fogas* (a pike-perch from Lake Balaton). Guests are serenaded with gypsy music.

Arany Kaviár ✿✿✿ *Ostrom utca 19; Tel. 201-6737.* Down the hill towards Moszkva tér, this small, cosy restaurant is a good place to sample generous portions of caviar with blinis at reasonable prices. The rest of the menu features standard Hungarian fare. Open for dinner only. No credit cards.

Aranyszarvas ✿✿ *Szarvas tér 1; Tel. 375-6451.* Long-established restaurant set in an elegant 17th-century house at the southern foot of Castle Hill. Famous for its game specialities; try the game paté pancakes and hare with bread dumplings.

Csalogány ✿✿ *Csalogány utca 26; Tel. 212-3795.* Specializing in traditional home-cooking, Csalogány is air-conditioned and accepts all credit cards. Open daily from 11am–11pm.

Fekete Holló ✿✿✿ *Országház utca 10; Tel. 356-2367.* Set on a relatively quiet part of this popular street, the Fekete Holló, (Black Raven) has a small, cheerful outdoor terrace—ideal for those windless summer days—or an attractive 18th-century dining room. If you want a truly exotic meal, try the pancakes with caviar followed by wild boar.

Fortuna Restaurant ✿✿✿ *Hess András tér 3; Tel. and fax 355-7177.* Try the house specialty of wild duck soup with saffron, or the stuffed peppers with lamb dumplings, or choose from Fortuna's variety of goulash dishes. Gypsy music.

Tabáni Kakas ✿✿ *Attila út 27; Tel. 375-7165.* Fowl is the speciality at Tabáni Kakas, considered one of the city's fashionable places to eat. It is conveniently situated behind Castle Hill. Everything from the chicken *(csirke)* to the stewed or stuffed turkey is cooked in goose fat. Guests can enjoy a peaceful atmosphere while listening to piano music (except Mondays).

ON AND AROUND RÓZSADOMB

Garvics ●●●● *Ürömi Köz 2; Tel. 326-3878.* Hungarian specialties grilled on volcanic tuffa rock. Credit cards accepted. Open Mondays through Saturday from 3pm–midnight. Closed on Sundays and holidays.

Mágnáskert ●● *Csatárka út 58; Tel. 325-9967.* Stylish new restaurant which bills itself as the premier business-dining venue of Buda; it has quickly built up a good reputation for its tasty Hungarian cuisine. Gypsy music. Terrace.

OBUDA

Kehli ●●●● *Mókus utca 22; Tel. 250-4241.* The Kehli is a small, wood-panelled local tavern with a long-standing gourmet tradition. For a truly different and delicious meal, start with bone-marrow, then try one of the house pork specials, and finish with a Transylvanian Golden Galushka pastry. Lovely summer courtyard. Accordion music. Closed Sunday.

Posta Kocsi ●●● *Fő tér 2; Tel. 368-7801.* The 18th-century coach house on Obuda's picturesque cobblestone square now serves tourists Transylvanian culinary delights: goose liver specialities. Gypsy music enhances the atmosphere. Formal attire.

Régi Sipos Halászkert ● *Nagy Lajos utca 46; Tel. 368-6480.* Not easy to find and rather low-key in a rustic way, but said to be the best value fish restaurant in town. (Its offspring on Obuda's Fő tér caters more for tourists, being smarter and considerably dearer.) Try the fish stew. Gypsy music. Closed Sunday.

Goldberg Söröző ●●● *Nagyszombat utca 6; Tel. 250-1573.* This beer hall offers curd cheese noodles and turkey specialties. All major credit cards accepted.

Budapest

Kerék ✿ *Bécsi út 103; Tel. 250-4261.* Expect this Austrian beer hall to serve up traditional Hungarian specialties such as goulash in a lively atmosphere of gypsy music. Credit cards accepted.

PEST—INNER CITY

Apostolok ✿✿ *Kigyó utca 4-6; Tel. 267-0290.* The Apostolok, housed in a converted 19th-century church, is rated as one of the most atmospheric eateries in the city. Typical Hungarian cuisine—try the mutton stew soup, pork cutlets ragout, or suckling pig with cabbage.

Kárpátia ✿✿ *Ferenciek tere 7-8; Tel. 317-3596.* Another tourist "must-see" restaurant with picturesque turn-of-the-century decor. Very reasonably priced Hungarian menu including some set-price meals. Try the turkey breast stuffed with ham and cheese. Gypsy music.

Kisitália ✿ *Szemere utca 22; Tel. 269-3145.* "Little Italy" is indeed a small place, with about eight tables. Service is quick and attentive. The Italian food is always reliable and there is a small drinks counter. The restaurant is closed Sundays.

Légrádi Testvérek ✿✿✿-✿✿✿✿ *Magyar utca 23; Tel. 318-6804.* One of the city's most fashionable eating places, offering an international/Hungarian menu for business types at lunch and well-to-do romantics at dinner. Oil paintings on its white walls and antique furniture make up the elegant decor. Food is served by tailcoated waiters on Herend china with silver cutlery. The atmosphere is quiet, with guitar music. The restaurant is air-conditioned. Closed weekends.

Mátyás Pince ✿✿✿ *Március tér 7; Tel. 318-1693.* One of Pest's favourite tourist spots serves good Hungarian dishes in an atmospheric turn-of-the century cellar setting. Those with a healthy appetite should try the King Matthias Platter. Gypsy music.

Ménes Csárda ❀❀❀ *Harmincad utca 4; Tel. 317-0803*. The Ménes Csárda is a famous, touristy restaurant, and as such, trades heavily on its folklore appeal. Try the roast leg of goose or the stuffed pork tenderloin. Gypsy music.

Claudia ❀❀ *Bástya utca 27; Tel.317-1983*. This first-class cellar restaurant serving Hungarian cuisine and specialties from the Mediterannean boasts an excellent wine selection. Open daily from 12pm until 12am. All major credit cards accepted.

Silhouette ❀❀❀❀ *Intercontinental Hotel, Apáczai Csere János utca 12-14; Tel. 327-6333*. Possibly the finest hotel restaurant in Budapest, the first-rate cuisine is complemented by splendid views of the Danube, luxurious decor, and impeccable service. The rack of lamb with sweetbreads is worth a try. The Silhouette is open daily for lunch from 12pm–3pm (except on Saturdays) and for dinner from 7pm–12am seven days a week.

Sörforrás ❀-❀❀ *Váci utca 15; Tel. 318-3814*. Despite its location and the mannequins outside, this isn't a tourist trap, but a well-run modern cellar restaurant serving good, authentic Hungarian dishes. Try loin of pork stuffed with cheese, ham, and mushrooms. Major credit cards accepted.

Százéves ❀❀❀❀ *Pesti Barnabás utca 2; Tel. 318-3608*. This elegant Baroque-style establishment is Budapest's most venerable restaurant and is still going strong after a century of business. Renowned for its game (try venison with cranberry sauce) and flambéed dishes. Summer terrace, gypsy music.

Szindbád ❀❀❀❀ *Markó utca 33; Tel. 332-2966*. Gourmet food for high flyers in a large cellar restaurant named after a character from Hungarian epicurean lore. Try a turkey speciality or the fine lamb dish with mint *(Báránycomb mentamártással)*. The Szindbád has an excellent selection of desserts and a spirit list.

Vegetárium ❀ *Cukor utca 3; Tel. 267-0322.* The city's first dedicated and best vegetarian restaurant offers a multi-ethnic, macrobiotic experience to please even the strictest vegans. Pleasant and relaxed New Age ambience with good service.

PEST—OUTSIDE THE INNER CITY

Bohémtanya ❀ *Paulay Ede utca 6; Tel. 322-1453.* At this aptly-named bohemian den you will always find half a dozen customers at the back at the bar, having a beer while they wait for a table. This busy and cramped *söröző* with a long menu of hearty and calorific local dishes is popular with locals and visitors on a tight budget. It serves large portions in a real beer-hall atmosphere. No credit cards.

Carmel ❀ *Kazinczy utca 31; Tel. 322-1834.* This spacious cellar restaurant is set in the heart of the Jewish Quarter, so it's not surprising that the long and interesting menu has a kosher flavour to it. Goose is the house speciality.

Fehér Bölény ❀❀❀❀ *Bánk utca 5; Tel. 312-2825.* The White Buffalo is famous for its steaks, regarded as the best not only in the city, but much farther afield as well. Kitschy American decor and country-and-western music. Dinner only.

Fészek Klub ❀ *Kertész utca 36; Tel. 322-6043.* The same genuine Budapest home-cooking menu as Kispipa (see below), but served in a pretty garden frequented by an arty crowd. Try the *"Reform" Bárány* (roast lamb). Club entry fee.

Gambrinus ❀❀❀ *Teréz körút 46; Tel. 153-0583.* This roomy, traditional restaurant provides a semi-formal setting for an interesting Hungarian/international menu. Go for the game or fish dishes, such as *fogas* fillets or hare in cream sauce. Gypsy music.

Kispipa ❀ *Akácfa utca 38; Tel. 342-2587*. Meaning small pipe, Kispipa is small, bright, and always crowded with locals, as well as a few adventurous tourists stumbling through an encyclopaedic, untranslated menu—which includes a number of (cheap) set-price meals. The venison with tarragon soup is excellent. Piano player. No credit cards. Closed Sunday. Reservations required.

Haxn Király Söráz ❀❀❀ *Király út 100; Tel. 351-6793*. Popular for its live folklore music in an Austro-Bavarian beer hall atmosphere, Haxn Király Söráz offers typical fare of pork knuckles and beer, goulash, and other Hungarian specialties. Open daily from 12pm–12am. All major credit cards accepted.

CITY PARK

Bagolyvár ❀ *Allatkerti út 2; Tel. 351-6395*. A branch of Gundel serving a very limited but superbly cooked range of Hungarian family-style dishes from a menu changing daily. Beautiful indoor dining room, lovely summer terrace. Possibly the best value in Budapest.

Gundel ❀❀❀❀ *Allatkerti út 2; Tel. 321-3550*. Situated near the zoo, the roar of lions often echoes in this restaurant. Gundel is a byword for Hungarian haute cuisine and the haunt of royalty, the super-rich, and well-heeled epicures. Recently revamped to its former palatial glory, it now features international as well as Hungarian gourmet delights. Be sure to save room for the dessert pancakes. Gypsy music. Reservations and formal dress required.

Robinson ❀❀❀ *Városliget; Tel. 343-0955*. The city's most idyllic and sylvan restaurant setting—on an island in the lake overlooking the leafy park. Excellent Hungarian and international cuisine in the restaurant, lighter meals served in café and grill (open April to September). Be sure not to miss the crêpes stuffed with vanilla cream and fresh fruit salad. Guitar music. Closed lunchtime weekends. Reservations and formal attire required.

ABOUT BERLITZ

In 1878 Professor Maximilian Berlitz had a revolutionary idea about making language learning accessible and enjoyable. One hundred and twenty years later these same principles are still successfully at work.

For language instruction, translation and interpretation services, cross-cultural training, study abroad programs, and an array of publishing products and additional services, visit any one of our more than 350 Berlitz Centers in over 40 countries.

Please consult your local telephone directory for the Berlitz Center nearest you or visit our web site at http://www.berlitz.com.

Helping the World Communicate